DEDICATION

For my Mother and Father

Ethel Newman and Thomas Newman

AGAINST THAT "POWERFUL ENGINE OF DESPOTISM"

The Fourth Amendment and General Warrants at the Founding and Today

Bruce A. Newman

University Press of America,® Inc.
Lanham · Boulder · New York · Toronto · Plymouth, UK

Copyright © 2007 by
University Press of America,® Inc.
4501 Forbes Boulevard
Suite 200
Lanham, Maryland 20706
UPA Acquisitions Department (301) 459-3366

Estover Road
Plymouth PL6 7PY
United Kingdom

All rights reserved
Printed in the United States of America
British Library Cataloging in Publication Information Available

Library of Congress Control Number: 2006934846
ISBN-13: 978-0-7618-3655-1 (paperback : alk. paper)
ISBN-10: 0-7618-3655-1 (paperback : alk. paper)

∞™ The paper used in this publication meets the minimum
requirements of American National Standard for Information
Sciences—Permanence of Paper for Printed Library Materials,
ANSI Z39.48—1984

This provision [the Fourth Amendment] seems indispensable to the full enjoyment of the rights of personal security, personal liberty, and private property. It is little more than the affirmance of a great constitutional doctrine of the common law.
Joseph Story, *Commentaries on the Constitution*

CONTENTS

PREFACE	ix
ACKNOWLEDGMENTS	xiii
INTRODUCTION	xv
CHAPTER 1: THE ORIGINAL UNDERSTANDING: THE COLONIAL EXPERIENCE	1
CHAPTER 2: THE PHILOSOPHY OF THE FOUNDERS	9
CHAPTER 3: SEARCH AND SEIZURE IN EARLY AMERICAN LAW	15
CHAPTER 4: SEARCHES IN PUBLIC AREAS: THE EARLY TWENTIETH CENTURY	31
CHAPTER 5: SEARCHES IN PUBLIC AREAS: THE LATE TWENTIETH CENTURY	47
CHAPTER 6: THE NEW DEAL AND COMMERCIAL SEARCHES	61

CONTENTS

CHAPTER 7: THE RISE OF THE ADMINISTRATIVE STATE AND THE RETURN OF THE GENERAL WARRANT ... 77

CONCLUSION ... 99

NOTES ... 107

BIBLIOGRAPHY ... 123

ABOUT THE AUTHOR ... 129

PREFACE

In one recent case, *City of Indianapolis v. Edmond*, the United States Supreme Court held that Indianapolis's vehicle check point program violated the Fourth Amendment by allowing suspicionless searches of vehicles for criminal evidence. While acknowledging that suspicionless searches have been held constitutional in certain situations, i.e., for the purpose of intercept illegal aliens (*United States v. Martinez-Fuerte*), for the purpose of operating sobriety *checkpoints* (*Michigan Dept. of State Police v. Sitz*), and for the purpose of conducting driver license and vehicle registration checks (*Delaware v. Prouse*), the Court held that suspicionless searches would not be considered constitutional if the primary purpose of the search was to detect evidence of criminal wrongdoing. In another recent case the court ruled that a vehicle checkpoint stop designed to gain information about a recent crime was constitutional because, for one thing, the primary purpose of the checkpoint was not to detect evidence of criminal wrongdoing. After *Edmond* and Lidster suspicionless stops of vehicles will be permissible where the primary purpose of the search is not criminal, while stops of vehicles of criminal suspects, must be based on probable cause. Criminal suspects are awarded more protection than law-abiding citizens.

These decisions illustrate a troubling propensity of the twentieth-century Court. The Court guards jealously (sometimes to the point of creating new rights) the protections available to criminal suspects, while at the same time is indifferent to the violations of the constitutional rights of law-abiding citizens. This is particularly true in the Court's Fourth Amendment jurisprudence. The Court has strengthened the protections of criminal suspects, for example, disallowing warrantless searches based on probable cause in public areas (roadways, sidewalks, etc.) although such searches took place at the time of the

Founding. At the same time, the Court allows the government to obtain a warrant to search commercial property (and sometimes homes) without demonstrating probable cause although the Fourth Amendment clearly requires a warrant. *Indianapolis v. Edmond* continues this tendency. Indeed, in *Edmond* the Court cites two cases discussed in this book, *Camera v. Municipal Court* (which allowed a suspicionless inspection of a home, and *Burger v. New York* (which allowed a suspicionless search of a junkyard).

In this book, I argue that the original understanding of the Fourth Amendment differentiated between searches on property and searches in public areas, generally requiring warrants to search property, while allowing warrantless searches in public areas if there was cause for the search. However, in the twentieth century this intent has been subverted. The government has weakened protections against searches of property, specifically commercial property, while expanding protections against searches in public areas.

This development arises from a change in the conception of justice among many political and legal thinkers. In the twentieth century these thinkers saw a need for an administrative state to control and regulate a vast economy that seemed to benefit only the wealthy.

The idea that government must increase the regulation of business led to a change in the judiciary's (and other government agencies) approach to commercial searches. The public interest, as defined by government agencies, began to take preference over businessmen's Fourth Amendment rights. So, for example, we got the administrative warrant, which is a warrant that does not require probable cause.

In the case of searches in public areas, the judiciary in the twentieth century has applied a much stricter standard than the Founding generation. The modern judiciary, with some retreat since the 1990's, has required warrants to search in public areas, while early jurists required only probable cause. This development is also due to a changed conception of justice, in which the modern judiciary has embraced a notion of liberty that emphasizes freedom divorced from morality. Furthermore, criminals come to be seen as the victims of society, in need of protection from the judiciary and other elites.

I argue that the Founder's understanding of justice and the importance of protecting property rights serve society better than the modern understanding of justice and our Fourth Amendment jurisprudence would be more just if we returned to the original understanding.

Bruce Newman
Altus, Oklahoma
22 August 2006

ACKNOWLEDGMENTS

IN AN ENDEAVER SUCH AS THIS THERE ARE SO MANY people to thank that one is always afraid that someone will be left out. To anyone inadvertently omitted let me now apologize.

This book is a revised version of my doctorial dissertation. Therefore I would like to thank my committee, Thomas G. West, Richard Dougherty, and Glen E. Thurow, not only for their support, but also for the many things I learned in their classes. It is a debt I will never be able to repay. I would like especially to thank Thomas West. Without his patience, encouragement and insight I doubt that this project could have been completed.

Most especially, I would like to thank my patient, understanding and wise wife, Alice. In so many ways she is truly a blessing, an underserved blessing, but one gratefully accepted.

INTRODUCTION

The right of the people to be secure in their persons, houses, papers and effects, against unreasonable searches and seizures, shall not be violated, and no Warrants shall issue, but upon probable cause, supported by Oath or affirmation, and particularly describing the place to be searched, and the persons or things to be seized.

- Fourth Amendment, United States Constitution

The exact meaning of these words of the Fourth Amendment has been the subject of great debate and much constitutional adjudication. For example, some scholars, like Akhil Amar, argue that the Fourth Amendment simply requires reasonable searches. The second clause of the amendment, the warrant clause, does not require—or even prefer—warrants in all but exigent circumstances, but simply spells out the procedures that must be obeyed if a warrant is issued. Even searches of property, if reasonable, do not require a warrant.[1] Other scholars, like Jacob Landynski, argue that the warrant clause is the dominant clause of the Amendment. According to this reading, the first clause of the amendment, the reasonableness clause, simply reemphasizes the requirement that only valid warrants be issued. A reasonable search is a search conducted under a warrant. Even searches in public areas require warrants.[2]

I argue that the original understanding of the Amendment differentiated between searches on property and searches in public areas, generally requiring warrants to search property, while allowing warrantless searches in public areas if there was cause for the search. Specifically, in this study, by examining the colonial history, the philosophy of the Founders, and the early practice after the adoption of the Constitution and the Bill of Rights, I will demonstrate that the Fourth

Amendment was primarily concerned with government searches of property. However, as I will show, in the twentieth century this intent has been subverted. The government has weakened protections against searches of property, especially commercial property, while expanding protections against searches in public areas.

The different interpretations of the Fourth Amendment arise from a change in the conception of justice among many political and legal thinkers. In the twentieth century they saw a need for an administrative state to control a huge economy that seemed to benefit only the wealthy. So John Dewey, an influential spokesman for this view, argues "Only by economic revision can the sound element in the older individualism—equality of opportunity—be made reality,"[3] and "socialized economy is the means of free individual development as the end."[4]

This idea, that government must extensively control and regulate business for the public good, led to a change in the judiciary's (and other government agencies) approach to commercial searches. The public interest, as defined by government agencies, begins to take preference over businessmen's Fourth Amendment rights. I will explore how, in recent decades, the warrant requirement is first ignored when it comes to commercial searches, and then gutted with the so-called "administrative warrant," which, like the "general warrant" of colonial times, allows government officials to obtain a search warrant without probable cause. The rise of the administrative state leads to the return of the general warrant.

In the case of searches in public areas, however, the judiciary in the twentieth century has applied a much stricter standard than did the Founding generation. The modern judiciary, with some modification in the 1990s, has required warrants for searches in public areas, while early jurists only required probable cause, and did not require officials to take the extra step of going to a judge and requesting a warrant. The officer, under the probable cause standard, could search in a public area without a warrant. But at the trial, he had to demonstrate probable cause to search, or he could be liable for damages. This development, I will argue, is also due to a changed conception of justice, in which the modern judiciary has embraced a notion of liberty that emphasizes freedom divorced from morality.

Since our privacy is understood to be more important than what we do with it, judges become more concerned about protecting the rights of suspected criminals in public areas. Therefore, they expanded protections requiring officials to get a warrant before searching in public areas.

INTRODUCTION   xvii

The original standard for searches was much different. The Founders wrote the Fourth Amendment in response to "writs of assistance," a form of general warrant that allowed British officers to search property without probable cause. The original understanding of the Fourth Amendment was to require warrants for the search of property, including commercial property. As I will show, the right to acquire and maintain property is key to the philosophy underlying the Founding. A system of private property helps check government by limiting its scope. There is a sphere of life that government must stay out of. This concern for property led the Founders to be more stringent regarding searches on property. Searches in public areas were a different story. If a person was in the public sphere and off his property, a warrant may have been impracticable, since the person might be able to escape apprehension. Thus "probable cause" was the original standard for searches in public areas. If an officer had probable cause he could search without a warrant. As the nineteenth century Pennsylvania Supreme Chief Justice Tilghman noted, to require a warrant for a search or seizure in a public area would endanger the safety of society.[5]

I intend to show that the Founder's understanding of justice and the importance of protecting property rights serve society better than the modern understanding of justice and privacy rights, and that our Fourth Amendment jurisprudence would be more just if we returned to the original understanding. The original understanding of the Fourth Amendment served the cause of justice by better protecting property owners from unjustified government intrusions onto their property and better preventing the guilty from going free than our modern understanding of the amendment. By making it harder to search property, but easier to search criminal suspects, the original understanding did a better job of both protecting the innocent and punishing (or at least discovering) the guilty.

CHAPTER 1

THE ORIGINAL UNDERSTANDING: THE COLONIAL EXPERIENCE

But Otis was a flame of fire! -- with . . . a torrent of impetuous eloquence, he hurried away every thing before him. American Independence was then and there born; the seeds of patriots and heroes were then and there sown . . . Every man of a crowded audience appeared to me to go away, as I did, ready to take arms against writs of assistance. Then and there was the first scene of the first act of opposition to the arbitrary claims of Great Britain. Then and there the child of Independence was born. In fifteen years, namely in 1776, he grew up to manhood, and declared himself free.[1]

To understand the character of the modern Supreme Court's Fourth Amendment jurisprudence we must first understand the original meaning of the Fourth Amendment. In this chapter I examine the origins of the amendment in the colonists' complaints about writs of assistance, complaints based on their understanding of natural rights and the common law. The colonists believed the writs violated their natural rights to property. The main purpose of the Fourth Amendment was to protect property by eliminating these writs of assistance.

The Colonists and Writs of Assistance

In 1696, the British Parliament passed a law allowing for the use of writs of assistance in the colonies. The writ was a form of a general warrant. Probable cause that the items searched for would be found in a particular place was not required. Under such a writ, officials could enter any place, including a house or place of business, and search for and seize prohibited goods. As Nelson Lasson puts it, "The writ empowered the officer and his deputies and servants to search at their will, wherever they suspected uncustomed goods to be, and to break open any receptacle or package falling under their suspecting eye."[2] The particular, or specific, warrants on the other hand, require particularized probable cause. The government official must go before a neutral magistrate and demonstrate to him that he has probable cause to find the goods he is looking for at the particular place he described. Then the judge decides if there is probable cause. If the officer has not demonstrated probable cause to search a particular place the judge is not supposed to issue the warrant. The warrant gives the added protection of having a magistrate decide the legitimacy of every search.

The writs of assistance were most often used in the colonies of Massachusetts and New Hampshire, and were used frequently to enforce revenue and custom laws.[3] A pernicious aspect of these writs of assistance is that they were not returnable after execution. Once issued they were good for the life of the sovereign—in fact, life and six months, not expiring until six months after the sovereign's death. Therefore, the power granted the official was almost unlimited. For the life of the sovereign the writs allowed the official to search wherever he suspected illegal goods were stored.[4]

James Otis first aroused the colonists against the writs of assistance. And, if John Adams's report quoted at the start of this chapter is to be believed, it was he who immediately gave birth to the movement for American independence. In 1760, King George II died, and in 1761 the writs of assistance expired. Sixty-three Boston merchants requested a hearing before the Superior court of Massachusetts on the question of renewing the writs. Arguing for the merchants and against the writs, Otis claimed that they were "instruments of slavery on the one hand, and villainy on the other," and that the writ was "the worst instrument of arbitrary power, the most destructive of English liberty, and the fundamental principles of the constitution, that ever was found in an English law book."⁵ Writs threatened liberty, he argued, because they violated the privileges of the home:

> One of the most essential branches of English liberty is the freedom of one's house. A man's house is his castle; and while he is quiet he is as well guarded as a prince in his castle. This writ, if it should be declared legal, would totally annihilate this privilege. Custom house officers may enter our houses when they please—we are commanded to permit their entry—their menial servants may enter—may break locks, bars and every thing in their way—and whether they break through malice or revenge, no man, no court can inquire—bare suspicion without oath is sufficient.⁶

Otis's main objection was that writs of assistance transgress upon the right of an English subject to be left alone in his house as long as he is not injuring anyone else. The home is the individual's castle, his realm; government officials should not enter while he is peaceful. To allow government officials to enter whenever they pleased would destroy the liberty man enjoys in his home. It would no longer be his castle.

Otis's argument is expanded in "The Rights of the Colonists and a List of Infringements and Violations of Rights," a pamphlet issued by the town of Boston in 1772, and largely written by Samuel Adams.⁷ Adams proclaims that the American colonists are endowed with natural rights, the most important of these being the rights to life, liberty, and property:

> Among the Natural Rights of the colonists are these First. a Right to Life: Secondly to liberty; thirdly to Property; together with the Right to support and defend them in the best manner they can⁸

According to Adams, the colonists possess rights not because they are Englishmen, but because they are human beings. These rights are not gifts of the government, but of God:

> It is the greatest absurdity to suppose it in the power of one or any number of men at entering into society, to renounce their essential natural rights, or the means of preserving those rights when the great end of civil government from the very nature of its institution is for the support, protection and defense of those very rights: the principal of which as is before observed, are life, liberty and property. If men through fear, fraud or mistake, should in terms renounce and give up any essential natural right, the eternal law of reason and the great end of society, would absolutely vacate such

renunciation; the right to freedom being the gift of God almighty, it is not in the power of Man to alienate this gift, and voluntarily become a slave.[9]

To paraphrase the Declaration of Independence, we are endowed by our *Creator* with certain unalienable rights, rights that are true and eternal. The British government owed the colonists the protection of their rights. Instead, they abused these rights. They abused these natural rights through, among other things, these general warrants known as writs of assistance:

> These Officers (revenue officers of the crown) are by their Commission invested with powers . . . to enter and go on board any Ship, Harbor, Creek or Haven, within limits of their commission; and also in the day time to go into any house, shop cellar, or any other place where any goods wares or merchandises lie concealed, or are suspected to lie concealed, whereof the customs & other duties, have not been, or shall not be duly paid . . . and the said house, shop, warehouse, cellar, and other place to search and survey, and all and every the boxes, trunks, chests and packs then and there found to break open.[10]

Again, we see the concern that general warrants allow government to invade indiscriminately a person's property. In this passage, Adams, unlike Otis, does not limit his complaint to invasion of the home, but argues that all property, including shops, warehouses and houses, should be protected against general warrants. Indeed many, if not most, of the complaints over writs of assistance came from businessmen and shopkeepers. These businessmen most often felt the blows of general warrants, as their businesses were searched for revenue violations under writs of assistance.[11] Under a general warrant, a man's property was subject to search (in the daytime) without a particularized warrant. Since the warrant protected the officer, an innocent person could not sue the officer for trespass. The general warrant treated the guilty and the innocent alike. The general warrant assumed that one's life, liberty and property were gifts of the state, not natural rights. What the state gave, the state could take away.

The point can be further developed by turning to James Wilson, one of the most important and influential political thinkers of late eighteenth century America. In his "Lectures on Law," Wilson explores Edmund Burke's understanding of the difference between civil and natural liberty. Burke argues that man cannot completely enjoy natural and civil rights together. When man enters civil society, he gives up his natural rights.[12] Wilson contends that the implication of this view is that under government people surrender their natural rights in return for "civil privileges."[13] A citizen's rights are seen as gifts of the government rather than gifts of God. If this view is correct, Wilson says, then "man is not only made *for*, but made *by* the government: he is nothing but what the society frames, he can claim nothing but what the society provides."[14] The purpose of good government, however, according to Wilson, is not the abridgment of natural rights, but rather the nourishment and protection of those natural rights, for "man's natural liberty, instead of being abridged, may be increased and secured in a government, which is good and wise. As it is with regard to his natural liberty, so it is with regard to his other natural rights."[15]

Since government is made for man, and not man for government, it is the duty of government to serve man. And that means protecting his natural rights. Rights are not something to use as barter – the government protects us in return for the surrender of some of our rights. Rather, good government protects and nourishes those rights.

The Founders wanted a government that protected and nourished natural rights, the rights—in the words of the Declaration of Independence—of life, liberty, and the pursuit of happiness. A good and wise government protects these rights, and since the British government did not do so, it was not a good and wise government. The concern that people such as Samuel Adams and James Otis had over writs of assistance was that they violated the rights to life, liberty and property

The Common Law

To understand the Fourth Amendment more fully we need to turn to the common law. According to Daniel Harris, "[t]he Fourth Amendment was adopted to constitutionalize the ... common law of search and seizure."[16] As Harris notes, Justice Story called the Fourth Amendment "little more than the affirmance of a great constitutional doctrine of the common law."[17]

The common law comprises rules of law developed by British judges, and sometimes modified by statutes, over centuries. Blackstone said that, among other things, the common law consisted of the general customs of England:

> the maxims and customs, so collected, are of higher antiquity than memory or history can reach (4): nothing being more difficult than

> to ascertain the precise beginning and first spring of an ancient and long established custom. Whence it is that in our law the goodness of a custom depends upon its having been used time out of mind: or, in the solemnity of our legal phrase, time whereof the memory of man runneth not to the contrary (5). This is that gives it its weight and authority: and of this nature are the maxims and customs which compose the common law, or lex *non scripta*, of this kingdom.[18]

Common law comes from customs so old that the origins have been forgotten. George Anastaplo states that the common law:

> reflects the everyday morality of the community, the applications of which is adjusted from case to case as justice and the common good require. It is developed primarily by judges, who find what is good and right to be done here and now, keeping in mind the known practices and expectations of the community. As such, the common law is indeed common—for it is understood to be law that would be generally accepted by common-law judges, whatever adjustments might be made for peculiar local conditions.[19]

The common law is related to natural law. As James Stoner has said:

> It had, after all, [at the time of the American revolution] long been a maxim at common law that it included nothing against reason and thus that it included natural law.[20]

James Wilson says that common law is "nothing else but common reason—that refined reason, which is generally received by the consent of all."[21] Blackstone also discusses natural law, stating that it is dictated by God and superior to any other. The natural law includes the principles that we should live honestly and hurt nobody, and render to everybody his due. Property also seems to be natural for Blackstone, as when he says that the "original of private property is probably founded in nature."[22] The natural law is the foundation of human law in that the human law is the attempt to put the principles of natural law into practice in a particular time and place.[23] Indeed, as one commentator notes, Blackstone's highest theme is the relation between natural law and conventional law. The same author states that for Blackstone "civil society consists of a set of conventional . . . rules and regulations whose purpose is the regularization and thereby the protection of natural rights.[24]

The common law was very important in the development of

American law. Justice Story has said that the common law became the fundamental law of the American colonies. Story says, "that the common law of England was emphatically the law of a free nation, and secured the public and private rights and liberties of the subjects against tyranny and oppression of the Crown."[25] Each colony adapted the common law to its own particular circumstances, but once:

> limited and defined by the colonists themselves, in its actual application, the common law became the guardian of their civil and political rights; it protected their infant liberties; it watched over their maturer growth; it expanded with their wants; it nourished in them that spirit of independence, which checked the first approaches of arbitrary power; it enabled them to triumph in the midst of dangers and difficulties; and by the providence of God, we, their descendants, are now enjoying, under its bold and manly principles, the blessings of a free and enlightened administration of public justice.[26]

The writs of assistance defied this common law tradition, one standard of which is that a man's home is his castle. Under common law, searches of premises generally required a particularized warrant.[27] Searches off premises, however, were treated differently. Any person, including a private person acting on his own accord, could search and seize at his peril, and if the search did not turn up evidence the person who had conducted the search could be sued for damages.[28] The common law, to use Daniel Harris' words, "drew a sharp distinction between searches of private premises and other kinds of searches [searches of people and vehicles in public areas]."[29] Writs of assistance were seen as an abuse because they allowed for searches of one's premises without probable cause.[30]

The purpose of common law is the protection of natural rights that had been abused in the state of nature.[31] As we have seen, this objective was partially achieved through protecting man's enjoyment of his property through preventing unjustified government intrusion on that property. It was this unjustified government intrusion on property that the Fourth Amendment was trying to prevent.

CHAPTER 2

THE PHILOSOPHY OF THE FOUNDERS

To understand the Founders' concern about searches and seizures one must consider the philosophy of the founding. This philosophy is best expressed in the Declaration of Independence. Among the four self-evident truths mentioned in the Declaration's famous second paragraph are the unalienable rights to life, liberty and the pursuit of happiness, which rights, the Declaration asserts, come not from man, but from the Creator. Since the rights are God-given, it is not up to the government to grant them, but rather it is the government's obligation to secure them for the people.

Property: "The Great Fence of Liberty"

The Founders believed that among one's natural rights was the right to property. The right to property is included among these natural rights as a part of the right to liberty. The Virginia Declaration of Rights of 1776 spells out the connection, stating that the "inherent rights" of man are "the enjoyment of life and liberty, with the means of acquiring and possessing property."[1] Alexander Hamilton, in his "Defense of the Funding System," stated that liberty "protect[s] the exertions of talent and industry and secures to them their justly acquired fruits."[2] In a 1795 Supreme Court case, the Court stated, "The right of acquiring and possessing property, and having it protected, is one of the natural, inherent, and unalienable rights of man."[3] In fact, the right to possess property is not just another natural right. As Thomas G. West has pointed out, it is the necessary condition of all other freedoms:

> Without private property, government would own the churches, printing presses and factories. Government would be able to dictate the practice of religion, speech, and employment, as it does under communism. For the Founders, property, as Edward J. Erler writes, is 'the great fence of liberty.'[4]

Property is a necessary, but not sufficient, condition of liberty. The system of private property helps to reduce the power of the government so that it does not control all aspects of a person's life. On his property, in his home, and in his private sphere (which includes his shop, his factory, his office, and his business), the individual man, not the government, is king. The Founders' doctrine of rights requires limited government: there is a realm of private life that government must respect and stay out of.[5]

Given this conception of the role of private property in a democratic society, we can see why the Founding generation was so concerned with general warrants, which allowed the British government to search private property indiscriminately. We can also see why the Founding generation was more concerned with searches in private areas—in homes, stores, warehouses and other buildings, where, as stated in the early New Hampshire case of *Jones v. Gibson*,[6] one has the exclusive right of possession and privacy—than searches in public areas. Government, when it allows searches of real property, invades that private realm. Government officials still had the right to search real (estate) property, for liberty did not mean license: if one was suspected of wrongdoing, the government did have the right to search one's property. However, because the government was invading a person's real property—that is, his private realm—in most cases officials had to go first to an impartial judge and demonstrate probable cause to be allowed to search. And they could not search until they secured a warrant from the judge. In public areas, on the other hand, warrants were not required before searching. But because of the importance of property to liberty and to republican government, a person had extra protection when on private property.

This connection between property rights and protection against unreasonable searches and seizures is succinctly stated by the eighteenth-century British jurist Lord Camden, in the famous search and seizure case *Entick v. Carrington:*

> our law holds the property of every man so sacred, that no man can set foot upon his neighbor's close without his leave; if he does he is a trespasser, though he does no damage at all, if he will tread upon his neighbor's ground he must justify it by the law.[7]

The right to real property is *sacred*. One's property is one's realm. No one, not even government officials, can enter that property, unless under the law. Government officials do not have an automatic right to invade one's property.

Liberty = License?

As I will show in Chapter 5, one reason modern Fourth Amendment jurisprudence becomes more protective of suspected criminals in searches in public areas, is the modern attempt to equate liberty with license, i.e., license to do what one pleases. Many of these searches in public areas involve drug possession. Drug possession is, in the view of many, a "victimless crime." As long as one is not hurting other one should the license to do as one pleases (See the discussion of *Memoirs v. Massachusetts* at the end of Chapter Five). One had natural rights, yet one did not have the right to do wrong. Alexander Hamilton wrote in 1775:

> To grant that there is a supreme intelligence who rules the world, and has established laws to regulate the actions of his creatures; and, still, to assert, that man, in a state of nature, may be considered as perfectly free from all restraints of law and government, appear to a common understanding, altogether irreconcilable.
> Good and wise men, in all ages, have embraced a very dissimilar theory. They have supposed, that the deity, from the relations, we stand in, to himself and to each other, has constituted an eternal and immutable law, which is, indispensable, obligatory upon all mankind, prior to any human institution whatever.
> This is what is called the law of nature....[8]

For Hamilton, even in the state of nature moral rules exist that a person must obey. James Wilson also makes this point. He argues in his "Law Lectures" that nature has furnished man with the impulse to seek his own happiness, and therefore he has the right to seek happiness *"provided he does no harm to others."*[9]

As Thomas G. West shows, many of the state constitutions written at the time of the Founding acknowledged the importance of promoting virtue. For example, the Pennsylvania Constitution stated, "Laws for the encouragement of virtue, and prevention of vice and immorality, shall be made and constantly kept in force, and provision shall be made for their due execution." The Massachusetts Constitution of 1780 said that "the happiness of a people, and the good order and preservation of civil government, essentially depend upon piety, religion, and morality." The Virginia Declaration of Rights of 1776 declared, "That no free government, or blessings of liberty, can be preserved to any people, but by a firm adherence to justice, moderation, temperance, frugality, and virtue."[10] The emphasis on inculcating virtue is probably best summed up by John Adams, the primary author of the Massachusetts Constitution of 1780, who states, "Without virtue, there can be no political liberty."[11]

As West points out, when the Founders spoke of self-government they meant that term in two senses:

> The Founders understood the term self-*government* in a double sense: (1) governing oneself morally, controlling one's tendency to indulge the selfish and violent passions unreasonably; and (2) governing oneself politically, through democratic institutions that provide a wide scope for self-governing private associations such as families, churches, private schools and businesses.
>
> The Founders therefore distinguished liberty from license and encouraged responsibility toward family and community.... They were far from taking for granted the moral character of the people.[12]

The right to liberty did not mean that moral transgressions would be permitted or excused. Self- government of the passions was necessary for self-government of the community to be successful. Therefore, the Founders had no objection to vigorously prosecuting wrongdoers. Those who used their natural liberty in harmful ways, and those who refused to govern themselves, were to be punished.

Contrast this with the twentieth-century interpretation of the Fourth Amendment, which makes it harder to conduct searches in public areas. The exclusionary rule, adopted by the U. S. Supreme Court in 1914, excludes evidence obtained by illegal search from criminal trials, even if the evidence clearly links the individual to the crime. The

THE PHILOSOPHY OF THE FOUNDERS 13

Founders did not have an exclusionary rule. Instead, they allowed all evidence, no matter how it was seized, into trial. For example, in the 1822 case of *United States v. La Jeune*, Justice Story, sitting as U. S. circuit court judge, stated:

> In the ordinary administration of municipal law the right of using evidence does not depend, nor, as far as I have any recollection, has ever been supposed to depend upon the lawfulness or unlawfulness of the mode, by which it is obtained. If it is competent or pertinent evidence, and not in its own nature objectionable, as having been created by constraint, or oppression, such as confessions extorted by threats or fraud, the evidence is admissible on charges for the highest crimes, even though it may have been obtained by a trespass upon the person, or by any other forcible and illegal means. The law deliberates not on the mode, by which it has come to the possession of the party, but on its value in establishing itself as satisfactory proof. In many instances, and especially on trials for crime, evidence is often obtained from the possession of the offender by force or by contrivances, which one could not easily reconcile to a delicate sense of propriety, or support upon the foundations of municipal law. Yet I am not aware, that such evidence has upon that account ever been dismissed for incompetency.[13]

As Massachusetts Supreme Court Justice Wilde notes, illegal searches were punished separately from the criminal trial:

> If the search warrant were illegal, or if the officer serving the warrant exceeded his authority, the party on whose complaint the warrant issued, or the officer, would be responsible for the wrong done; but this is no good reason for excluding the papers seized as evidence, if they were pertinent to the issue . . . . When papers are offered in evidence, the court can take no notice how they were obtained, whether lawfully or unlawfully; nor would they form a collateral issue to determine that question.[14]

Under the old standard, then the officer was held responsible for violating the suspect's Fourth Amendment rights through civil suits. The criminal defendants could sue the officer for damages, alleging trespass or false imprisonment.[15] But, as we see from the above statements, the evidence was still used in trial.

Because of the fear that a suspected criminal could flee before officials were able to locate a judge to obtain a warrant, and because the suspect was not on his property, the Founding generation did not require a warrant to conduct searches in public areas. If the officer had reasonable or probable cause, he could conduct a search on the spot. The prohibition against unreasonable searches and seizures was meant to protect the innocent from unwarranted governmental intrusion, not to hinder law enforcement. Not confusing liberty with license, the Founding generation allowed warrantless searches in public areas, if they were conducted with cause.

CHAPTER 3

SEARCH AND SEIZURE IN EARLY AMERICAN LAW

As we saw in the Introduction, Fourth Amendment scholar Akil Amar argues that the warrant clause of the amendment does not implicitly require warrants for most searches.[1] The warrant requirement, in Amar's view, is instead a limitation on warrants, stipulating that officials who use warrants must meet the requirements spelled out in the amendment. Amar argues that there is not one antebellum case that recognizes an implicit warrant requirement.[2] This is true. However, the antebellum cases I examined involved searches outside of buildings, and (as I have discussed) searches in public areas did not require warrants at that time. Furthermore, Amar argues that the congressional laws of the nineteenth and twentieth century did not require warrants to search buildings, but only provided for warrants as an option. Amar cites the Collections Act of July 31, 1789, to argue that the provision that authorizes warrants to search houses, buildings, stores, etc., merely *entitles*, but does not *require*, warrants to search those places.[3] If this were true, though, why would one differentiate between searches on ships and searches of buildings, as the act does? Why doesn't the act say simply that the officer has the right to search any building or vessel without a warrant? A clear reading of the statute, it seems to me, is that it requires warrants for the search of places.[4] This distinction is clearly shown in another early law of Congress, An Act Further to Provide for the Collection of Duties.[5] The act allows officers to search any vehicle or carriage for illegally imported goods, but states that an officer is entitled to a warrant for the search of any dwelling-house, store or other building. To the authors of this act, passed just twenty-four years after the Bill of Rights was ratified, the clear implication of the phrase "entitled to" is that a warrant is necessary, not optional. For the statute declares that the *necessity* of a search warrant arising under the act (to search homes, stores, etc.) should in no case be applied to the searches of vehicles and carriages.[6] The only time search warrants are mentioned in the act is in the reference to searches of buildings, so in talking about the necessity of a search warrant the authors of the act are obviously stating that a warrant is necessary to search buildings. Amar is right to suggest that Supreme Court Fourth Amendment jurisprudence in the twentieth century is not the highlight of the Court's work,[7] but he is wrong to suggest that the problem is with the Court's emphasis on the warrant clause in all situations, since the Founding generation did not require warrants in all situations.

Jacob Landynski argues, in contrast, that the original understanding required warrants both on private premises and in public areas except in emergency circumstances. In his criticism of Chief Justice Taft's majority opinion in *Carroll v. United States*[8] (a case that upholds the warrantless search of a vehicle), Landynski claims that warrantless searches were only allowed at entry points into the United States:

> Taft's use of history was faulty and did not prove his point, for the reason that the long-standing congressional approval of search of vessels without warrant sanctioned only a hunt for goods entering the United States on which duty had not been paid, not for evidence to be seized domestically for use in a criminal prosecution. In the words of Professor Black, "Congress has the authority to require every vehicle to stop and be subjected to search at an international boundary when the occupant thereof is seeking admission into the country, even in the absence of any suspicion or probable cause." [9]

I would argue that it is not Taft's historical interpretation that is faulty, but rather Landynski's and Black's. In this chapter I will look at a number of search and seizure cases from the early days of our country. These cases involve warrantless searches in public areas, which were upheld as legal. As I shall show, the customs laws that allow for warrantless searches outside of private property do not specify that these warrantless searches can occur only at international borders. The record shows Landynski and Black to be wrong; early American law did allow domestic warrantless searches in public areas.

The Early State Constitutions

The concern over writs of assistance led many states to outlaw these writs in the state constitutions that were written after the Revolution. *Eight of the early states had bills of rights,*[10] and *all of these* protected against general warrants.[11] Four of the state bills of rights (those of Pennsylvania, Vermont, New Hampshire and Massachusetts) also contained statements against unreasonable searches and seizures; but the wording was such, as Nelson Lasson points out, that it is clear that the unreasonable search or seizure thus targeted is the one conducted by a general warrant.[12] The first constitutional guarantee against general warrants was found in Section 10 of the June 12, 1776 Virginia Declaration of Rights:

> That general warrants, whereby any officer or messenger may be commanded to search suspected places without evidence of a fact committed, or to seize any person or persons not named, or whose offence is not particularly described and supported by evidence, are grievous and oppressive, and ought not to be granted.[13]

This Declaration of Rights, which is typical of the other state constitution's statements on search and seizure, condemns general warrants because they allow a person's property or person to be invaded without the support of evidence. Since only mere suspicion is required, they in effect allow anyone's property or person to be searched and seized. These warrants are indiscriminate, and as such they infringe upon a person's natural right to liberty and property. It is also important to note that the complaint in the Virginia Declaration of Rights is directed against general warrants. All searches, even warrantless searches under some circumstances, are not condemned. It is the indiscriminate searches under the authority, and hence protection, of general warrants that are prohibited.

Search and Seizure and the Ratification of the Constitution

General warrants were also an issue in the debate over the ratification of the U.S. Constitution. Many of the opponents of the original Constitution were concerned that it lacked a bill of rights. Samuel Bryan, in the Antifederalist essay "Centinel I," argued that the Penn sylvania Ratifying Convention would decide the fate of the liberties of Pennsylvanians. Ratifying the proposed new Constitution would be a mistake, he claimed, because it would set up a permanent aristocracy and did not protect the liberties of the citizens. Under the Pennsylvania Constitution 1 was protected against unreasonable searches and seizures, but under the Constitution one's house would no longer be one's castle, and one's person and property would not be held free from general warrants.[14] The "Letter #4 from a Federal Farmer," argued that a federal bill of rights was needed to protect, among other essential rights, the "freedom from hasty and unreasonable search warrants, warrants not founded on oath, and not issued with due caution, for searching and seizing men's papers, property, and persons."[15] At the Pennsylvania Ratifying Convention Robert Whitehill proposed a series of amendments to the federal Constitution. Among those amendments was one that stated that "warrants unsupported by evidence . . . are grievous and oppressive, and shall not be granted either by the magistrates of the federal government or others."[16] The New York, Maryland, Virginia and North Carolina conventions all passed resolutions urging that a bill of rights be added to the federal Constitution, and that the bill of rights contain prohibitions against general warrants.[17] The Founding generation considered general warrants breaches of the natural rights of man, and wanted to make sure that the new federal government did not make use of them.

While all the men cited above were Antifederalists, I do not mean to imply that only the Antifederalists were worried about general warrants. *The supporters of the Constitution did not complain of a lack of a specific prohibition against general warrants because they favored these warrants.* Rather, they thought a bill of rights was unnecessary and harmful. They thought, to paraphrase Alexander Hamilton in *Federalist Paper 84*, that the Constitution itself was a bill of rights, and as such protected the people's natural rights through the mechanisms of separation of powers, checks and balances, and the federal system with its explicit delegation of authority to the national government. A bill of rights was a mere "parchment barrier," worth only the paper it was written on, and the inclusion of a bill of rights in the constitution might suggest that the rights listed were the only rights the people had, and so imply that the federal government had more power than it really should.

The Fourth Amendment

Nevertheless, soon after the first Congress convened in 1789, Congressman James Madison introduced his proposed amendments to the Constitution—amendments that would create a federal bill of rights. One proposed amendment stated that:

> The rights of the people to be secured in their persons; their houses, their papers, and their other property, from all unreasonable searches and seizures, shall not be violated by warrants issued without probable cause, supported by oath or affirmation, or not particularly describing the places to be searched, or the persons or things to be seized.[18]

Madison's proposed amendment is one flowing statement. It simply says that the rights of the people to be secure in their persons and homes shall not be violated by warrants issued without cause, i.e., general warrants. It is quite clear that general warrants are the mischief being aimed at here. The final version[19] splits the amendment into two clauses[20] -- the reasonableness clause, which states that all searches must be reasonable, and the warrant clause, which delineates the procedures a government official must follow in obtaining a proper warrant. How are the two clauses related? I have already indicated that the colonists' complaints were directed towards general warrants, not warrantless searches. Their argument was not that all searches were wrong, but that indiscriminate searches violated the natural rights to liberty and property, if not life, by assuming that a man's property could be searched at will by the state.

The Fourth Amendment was aimed not at limiting all warrantless searches, but indiscriminate ones. The Founders stipulate that government officials must appear before a judge and demonstrate probable cause to search before invading someone's property, but they did not condemn warrantless searches in public areas, of property and persons, as long as there was cause. Indeed, many warrantless searches took place at the time of the Founding and for many years thereafter.[21] This is especially true for searches incident to arrest.[22] The Founders did not want to hamper law enforcement.

Early State Statutes

Before the establishment of the Constitution, many states had written into statutory law the common law preference for warrants to search premises and for warrantless searches in public areas. During the revolutionary period some states passed laws aimed at preventing trade with Britain. For example, a New Jersey statute read:

> That it shall and may be lawful for any Person or Persons to seize any Goods, Wares or Merchandise, that shall be discovered coming out of the Lines or Encampments of the Enemy or of their adherents, or that shall be brought out of any Place in their actual Power of Possession in this or the adjacent States, or that may be found in or passing through this State, together with the Boats, Carriages, Teams and Horses conveying the same....
>
> AND BE IT FURTHER ENACTED *by the Authority aforesaid*, That it shall and may be lawful for any Judge of the court of Common-Pleas in any county of this State, and he is hereby authorized and required, upon Application to him made, and due and satisfactory Cause of Suspicion shown, on Oath or affirmation, which Oath or Affirmation shall be taken in Writing and subscribed, as in case of stolen Goods, that Goods, Wares or Merchandise, liable to Seizure by Virtue of this Act, are concealed or deposited in any Dwellinghouse or other Building whatsoever, within such County, to grant a Warrant, directed to the Sheriff or any of the Coroners of such County, who are hereby respectively required to pay Obedience to such Warrant, and to make Search for, and to seize and secure such Goods, Wares or Merchandise; and in case of Refusal to permit such Search, or if Opposition be made thereto, to break open Doors and Locks for the Purpose aforesaid. PROVIDED ALWAYS, That no such search shall be made before Sun-rising, nor after Sun-setting. AND PROVIDED ALSO, That no person shall be hereby authorized to enter any House or other Building as aforesaid, other than the Sheriff or Coroner, and two respectable Freeholders not being the Informers, or interested in the Seizure, unless Opposition be made by an armed Force.[23]

We see in this law that the state is much more lenient toward searches outside one's premises. According to this act, someone can seize illegal goods passing through the state at will, while seizing goods on someone's premises, in a building or a house, require a warrant. Notice the care that goes into issuing and serving the warrant. "Due and satisfactory cause of suspicion" must be established before the warrant is issued, the search can only be undertaken during daytime hours, and the only persons who can enter the building are the sheriff or coroner and two "respectable freeholders." Pennsylvania and New York also had laws that distinguished between searches on roads or in open areas, and searches on property.[24] As is common in the Founding period, the drafters of these laws show great respect for real property, while giving the state greater leeway in searches off one's property.[25]

Federal Search and Seizure Case Law

The Fourth Amendment case law at the federal level is sparse prior to the Twentieth Century. Congress passed a few statutes dealing with searches and seizures, usually—but not exclusively—in customs cases; but very few of the laws (many of which I will discuss later) were challenged in the Supreme Court. Congress exercised limited criminal jurisdiction. Crime was considered a local matter to be handled by the states as part of their police power.[26] Only one Fourth Amendment case, *Ex Parte Burford* involved an improperly issued warrant.[27]

Of the Fourth Amendment cases the Supreme Court did hear, *The Apollon*,[28] and *Locke v. United States*[29] bear close inspection. *Locke* is important because here John Marshall gives his famous definition of probable cause. He states,

> that the term 'probable cause,' according to its usual acceptation, means less than evidence which would justify condemnation; and, in all cases of seizure, has a fixed and a well-known meaning. It imports a seizure made under circumstances that warrant suspicion. In this, its legal sense, the court must understand the term to have been used by Congress.[30]

Probable cause does not require enough evidence to convict, but simply enough to provide reasonable suspicion. In fact, the terms *probable* and *reasonable cause* at the time of the Founding "meant 'probable cause to suspect.'"[31]

The more interesting of the two cases is the *Apollon*. The ship *Apollon* was seized by an American port collector at St. Joseph's, across the St. Mary's River from Georgia. St. Joseph's was at the time in Spanish territory, and the Apollon was searched for failing to report to the port master, as every ship arriving in the U. S. was required to do by law. Ruling on the case, Justice Story found that the ship had been illegally searched and its cargo illegally seized by U.S. customs officers. He states that the St. Mary's is an international river and since the ship was only traveling on the river, and not stopping at U. S. ports, the seizure was illegal. Story sustains, with minor exceptions, the damages awarded to the shipowners by lower courts. This case shows that the old remedy for illegal searches and seizures worked. Although this discussion concerns the substantive issue of the correct meaning of the

Fourth Amendment and not the remedial issue of how to punish violations of the Fourth Amendment, it is interesting to compare how violations of the Fourth Amendment were remedied at the time of the founding, with how they are remedied in the twentieth century. In early American jurisprudence, when a person or thing was seized illegally the remedy was a suit for trespass or false imprisonment.[32] The evidence seized illegally was not excluded from the trial. Following the common law standard, all evidence that is pertinent to the case is used, no matter how the evidence is obtained.[33] This standard changed in the early twentieth century, when Iowa adopted the exclusionary rule in 1903 and the United States Supreme Court adopted the exclusionary rule for federal cases in 1914.[34] The exclusionary rule requires that evidence seized illegally be excluded from trial. Many argue today that the we must have the exclusionary rule because there must be a remedy for illegal searches, and that the only real alternative, tort suits, will not work because no jury will find against a (usually) respectable police officer and for a (usually) rather disagreeable criminal who is the victim of an illegal search. Yet, under the old standard, both victims of illegal searches and society were protected. Victims of illegal searches could sue the people who conducted the search and win damages. But the evidence could still be used in court. A guilty man would not go free because the evidence was excluded. Under the modern remedy the evidence of an illegal search, no matter how convincing it is, cannot be used in court. Society is punished, then, as evidence that could be used to convict a suspect is excluded, and may enable the suspect to go free. As Benjamin Cardozo wrote while serving on the New York State bench, under the exclusionary rule, "The criminal is to go free because the constable has blundered."[35]

State Case Law

Because of the paucity of search and seizure cases at the federal level in the early days of the republic, it is important to turn to state cases to understand the beliefs of early Americans on the issue of search and seizure. One of the most important cases involves a seizure, that is, an arrest of a person, not a search. In *Wakely v. Hart*,[36] a case brought before the Pennsylvania Supreme Court, Wakely appealed his arrest and subsequent conviction on the charge of larceny. He had been arrested without a warrant and taken to jail where the stolen item, a watch, was found on his person.[37] Wakely contested his arrest because it violated the Pennsylvania Constitution's warrant requirement, and he sued for trespass and assault and battery. The court rejected his appeal and ruled for the defendant, Hart. In delivering the opinion of the court Chief Justice Tilghman said that the Pennsylvania Constitution's warrant clause is aimed at general warrants and nowhere prohibits an arrest without a warrant:

> The provisions of this section (Pa. Con. art. 9, sec.7), so far as concerns warrants, only guard against their abuse by issuing them without cause, or in so general and vague a form, *as may put it in the power of the officers who execute them to harass innocent persons under pretence of suspicion*: for if general warrants are allowed, it must be left to the discretion of the officer, on what persons or things they are to be executed. But it is nowhere said, that there shall be no arrest without warrant. To have said so would have endangered the safety of society.[38]

The warrant clause in question, then, according to Tilghman, is not an endorsement of warrants, but a limitation on them. To argue otherwise, by insisting that all arrests must be made with a warrant, endangers rather than protects the innocent. All of society is endangered when the guilty go free. The felon who is caught red-handed, who is seen committing a crime, may be arrested and searched without a warrant. He must be arrested on the spot or he may escape – and possibly commit another crime. Tilghman further argues that if a person is not seen, but is known by other means to have committed a felony, the person may be pursued with or without a warrant. Even a private person may arrest, at his peril, a felon on probable cause of suspicion, with or without a warrant.[39] The criminal suspect must be convicted, or the seizure is not justified and the private individual is liable for damages even if he had probable cause for the seizure. The officer, on the other hand, is justified by probable cause.[40] These above-stated points are principles of common law, Tilghman says, and were not meant to be changed by the warrant clause of the constitution:

> The whole section (Pa. Con. Art. 9, sec. 7) indeed, was nothing more than an affirmance of the common law, for general warrants have been decided to be illegal; but as the practice of issuing them had been ancient, the abuses great and the decisions *against them* only of modern date, agitation occasioned by the discussion of this important question had scarcely subsided, and it was thought prudent to enter a *solemn veto* against this powerful engine of despotism.[41]

The Founding generation was so concerned about these general warrants that they enumerated in the federal and many state constitutions prohibitions against these "engines of despotism."

Wakely concerns warrantless arrest in a public area. What about warrantless searches? There are a number of cases concerning warrantless searches in public areas from the Founding period. *Sailly v. Smith* is an 1814 case that involves a warrantless search of a public horse shed.[42] Smith was a customs collector for the district of Champlain in New York. He seized certain dry goods belonging to Sailly from a sleigh in an open public horse shed standing by a public highway. The dry goods had been imported into the country from Great Britain in violation of a statute of Congress.[43] Sailly sued for damages, claiming that the seizure was a trespass, since no warrant for seizure of the goods had been issued.[44] The court ruled for the defendant Smith. Judge Yates, delivering the opinion of the court, ruled that since the goods were in a public shed the collector did not need a warrant. "The collector . . . had a right by law (the statute of Congress) to make the seizure, and to retain the goods in his custody, until it could be ascertained, by due course of law, whether they were forfeited or not."[45] The statute, The Act to Interdict the Commercial Intercourse between the United States and Great Britain and France of 1811, allowed customs officers to seize goods imported into the United States contrary to the intent of the act, until trial could ascertain whether or not the goods had been imported illegally and, therefore, should be forfeited to the United States.[46] Yates does not even feel the need to argue for his finding. He takes it for granted that anyone reading the decision will realize that since the goods were found in a public area no warrant was needed to seize them. This is strong evidence in favor of the view that warrants were not considered necessary for all searches by the Founding generation.

Jones v. Gibson[47] also involves a warrantless search in a public area. In *Jones* a customs inspector took items from a stagecoach, items that he suspected had been illegally imported to the United States. After taking the goods, he stored them in the house of Mr. Gibson, with Gibson's consent. Later, Gibson gave the goods to persons claiming to be the owners. The custom inspector sued Gibson for trespass for taking the goods, arguing that the goods, by virtue of his federal commission, belonged under his control.[48]

One of the issues in this case is whether the customs inspector could legally lay claim to the goods, and therefore have standing to sue Gibson for taking them. Gibson's lawyers argued that the inspector did not legally have a claim to the goods because he seized them from a stagecoach without a warrant, and the act under which the inspector seized the goods required him to have a warrant when searching a house, building or "other place." Gibson's lawyers claimed that the words "other place" include stagecoaches, thus making it illegal to seize the goods without a warrant.[49]

The court ruled against Gibson. It said the words "other place" in the statute did not mean other place in the most general sense of the words. For in the "general sense of words, every material object must occupy such place." In other words, in the general use of the words "other place" the search of all places no matter where or what they were, be they vessels, stage coaches, other vehicles or barns could not be conducted without a warrant. There would be no exceptions to the search warrant under this interpretation of the statute. If the legislature had intended this, the court argues, the statute would have stated simply that no searches may be conducted without a warrant. Instead, the statue specifies that a warrant was required to search dwelling houses, stores, buildings, or other places. Therefore, the court rules that the phrase "other place" refers to places substantially the same as the places mentioned before. It meant to prohibit the warrantless searches of other structures.[50] These buildings were intended to have extra protection:

> This prohibition of entering certain places for the purpose of searching for and seizing goods without a magistrate's warrant was clearly intended to guard individuals against improper intrusion into their buildings where they had the *exclusive* right of possession and privacy, under the pretext of searching for goods subject to seizure, and the words, "other place" means other place, where the occupant has this exclusive right of possession and privacy.[51]

Real property is treated differently than other types of property. Real property, including houses and stores, receive extra protection because the owner has the *exclusive* right of possession there. They are the individual man's realm, not the government's. Therefore, if government is to intrude on that property, special justification is needed. The government intrusion must be reasonable, meaning that a judicial officer must approve a warrant for a search; and the officer must make an oath or affirmation before the judicial officer before the warrant will be granted.

In public areas, or on public roads, one is not on one's property and the standard for legal searches is lower. Warrantless searches are justifiable in those areas. In *Jones v. Gibson* the warrantless search was of a passenger in a stagecoach:

> A passenger in a stagecoach has no such exclusive right of possession, as is contemplated in this provision of the act, he has only a right in common with others, only a right to the spot he occupies so long as he continues to occupy it. That this is the true construction of this provision of the law is assumed as the ground of decision in the case of *Sailly v. Smith*, 11 Johns. Rep. 500. That was an action of trespass against a collector for seizing goods imported contrary to law, from a sleigh standing in an open shed, without a warrant. And the court decided that a warrant was not necessary.[52]

The court, citing *Sailly v. Smith*, reinforces the point made earlier that a warrantless search outside a home or place of business is not necessarily illegal or unconstitutional. The early Americans' concern did not involve warrantless searches in public areas or on public roads. As long as these searches were based on cause, they were considered legal and proper. Their chief concern was over general warrants that allowed the search of all homes and businesses based on little or no suspicion, and which were understood to constitute an unjustified violation of property rights by the government.

For further evidence that searches in public areas did not require warrants, I will turn to the Massachusetts case of *Jones v. Root*.[53] In this case a West Springfield selectman stopped a wagon illegally transporting liquor. The selectman was acting under a Massachusetts statute that authorized:

> any mayor, alderman, selectman . . . in his city or town without a warrant, [to] arrest any person or persons whom they may find in the act of illegally selling, transporting or distributing intoxicating liquors, and seize the liquors vessels and implements of sale in the possession of said person or persons, and detain them in some place of safekeeping.[54]

The question in the case was not whether the stop and seizure of the wagon was legal, but whether the selectman could store the wagon transporting the liquor in his barn until the owner (who was not driving the wagon) arrived to pick it up. The court ruled that the statute did not violate the state constitution, and that the selectman did not appropriate Jones's goods for his own use by storing the horses at his stable. Here an early state court again upholds a warrantless search and seizure in a public area.

Congressional Search and Seizure Statutes

Another way of establishing the original understanding of the Fourth Amendment is to look at the laws the early Congresses passed concerning search and seizure. Most of these laws, like the ones involved in *Sailly* and *Jones,* concerned customs. The same Congress that proposed what eventually became the Fourth Amendment passed three customs acts that bear on our question. The first, The Collections Act of 1789, empowers federal officers to search for goods imported into the United States without duty:

> every collector naval officer and surveyor, . . . shall have full power and authority, to enter any ship or vessel, in which they shall have reason to suspect any goods, wares or merchandise subject to duty shall be concealed; and therein to search for, seize, and secure any such goods, wares or merchandise; and if they shall have cause to suspect a concealment thereof, in any particular dwelling-house, store, building, or other place, they . . .upon application on oath or affirmation to any justice of the peace, be entitled to a warrant to enter such house, store, or other place (in the day time only) and there to search for such goods, and if any shall be found, to seize and secure the same for trial. [55]

The officers can search ships and vessels without a warrant if they have "reason to suspect" such a ship or vessel contains contraband goods. The authors of this act consider such a warrantless search reasonable. However, even here the officers must have reasonable suspicion to search. They cannot just search a ship or vessel arbitrarily. Notice, when it comes to homes, stores or *any* particular buildings the officer must go before a justice of the peace, give an oath or affirmation and secure a warrant. The members of this First Congress obviously did not consider a warrant necessary for all searches; but also they believed that private buildings were entitled to extra protection from government searches. To search these private buildings a warrant was needed.[56]

As James Etienne Viator has pointed out, the Collection Act became law less than a month before Madison proposed his search and seizure amendment to the U. S. Constitution. The same Congress that proposed the Fourth Amendment passed more than one act that allowed warrantless searches outside of buildings, but required a warrant to search buildings:

> Hence, because the same legislators were busy working on both proposals, it is not unreasonable to assume that the sorts of

searches detailed in the Collection Act provide persuasive evidence of what search and seizure techniques were considered to be reasonable within the meaning of the Fourth Amendment."[57]

Viator nicely explains the distinction between searches of buildings and other searches found in the Collection Act of 1789:

> the Collection Act of 1789, therefore, should be enough in and of itself to refute anyone who argues that, at least by the original understanding, the reasonableness clause of the Fourth Amendment should be read in tandem with the warrant clause of the Fourth Amendment to declare that the only reasonable searches countenanced by the Fourth Amendment's congressional enactors were those proceeded under a warrant... the Collection Act paid homage to the traditional English axiom that "a man's home is his castle" by providing that any search of a building—and, notice, not just a house but a store or other building—was to proceed under a warrant given on oath or affirmation and particularly describing the location to be searched.[58]

The passage of the Collection Act by the First Congress argues against the position of Landynski and others that the Fourth Amendment allows only searches conducted by a warrant. As Viator correctly emphasizes, the Collection Act did not give special protection to homes, but provided protection to all privately owned buildings.[59]

The Collection Act was not the only law that First Congress passed requiring warrants to search places. There was, for example, a law entitled An Act Repealing Duties (1 Stat. 199, 1791). This act provides that if a federal officer suspects that spirits are being hidden in places with the intent of evading duties on said spirits the officer may apply to a judge or justice for a warrant to search such places.[60] This act says nothing about searches outside of places, and says nothing about warrantless searches. However, again we see that a warrant is required for a search in a place.[61] The authors do not specify what they mean by place, but based on the way the term is used in both the Fourth Amendment and the custom law described above, we can be fairly sure that by place they mean building, that is a store or a house, and not a vessel or other vehicle.

The third act I want to consider is An Act Further to Provide for the Collection of Duties (3 Stat. 231, 1815). This act is similar to the first act described. It requires a search warrant to search any house, store or other building for goods unlawfully imported into the United States. It provides for warrantless searches outside of buildings:

it shall be lawful for any collector, naval officer, surveyor, or inspector of the customs . . . to stop, search, and examine any carriage or vehicle, of any kind whatsoever, and to stop any person traveling on foot, or beast of burden, on which he shall suspect there be any goods, wares, or merchandise, which are subject to duty, or which shall have been introduced into the United States in any manner contrary to law; and if such officer find any goods, wares, or merchandise, on any such carriage, vehicle, person travelling on foot, or beast of burden, which he shall have probable cause to believe are subject to duty, or shall have been unlawfully introduced into the United States, he shall seize and secure the same for trial.[62]

In this statute the customs officer is only allowed to seize items if there is probable cause to suspect that the items have been illegally imported into the United States. Nevertheless, when it comes to buildings a warrant is required for a search:

if any of the said officers of the customs shall suspect that any goods . . . which are subject to duty, . . . are concealed in any particular dwelling house, store, or other building, he shall, upon proper application, on oath, to any judge or justice of the peace, be entitled to a warrant, directed to such officer, who is hereby authorized to serve same, to enter such house, store, or other building, in day time only, and here to search and examine whether there are any goods, . . . which are subject to duty.[63]

Again, we see a double standard. Buildings, including homes and stores, receive extra protection under the statute. And it is not only homes, but also places of business, stores, that receive the extra protection of a warrant requirement. Following this clause requiring a warrant to search a Building, Congress reiterates that a warrant is not to be required to search in vehicles or public areas:

Provided always, That the necessity of a search warrant, arising under this act, shall in no case be considered as applicable to any carriage, wagon, cart sleigh, vessel, boat, or other vehicle, of whatever form or construction, employed as a medium of transportation, or to packages on any animal or animals, or carried by man on foot.[64]

Congress feels so strongly about the right to search vehicles and persons on foot without a warrant that it adds a clause to this section of the statute specifically stating that although all searches in buildings are to be conducted by warrants, this should not be interpreted to mean that warrants are required for searches in vehicles or public areas. There could be no clearer evidence that the early Americans did not believe that the Fourth Amendment set out an absolute warrant requirement. The Fourth Amendment obviously was not meant by the early generations to require a warrant in all situations.[65]

CHAPTER 4

SEARCHES IN PUBLIC AREAS: THE EARLY TWENTIETH CENTURY

As we saw in the previous chapters, the original understanding of the Fourth Amendment allowed for warrantless searches in public areas, but required warrants to search places. As the twentieth century wore on, however, this original understanding was gradually discarded. Twentieth-century jurisprudence moved towards a warrant requirement for searches in public areas and away from this earlier understanding that allowed warrantless searches. An example of this development is seen in an article by Joseph D. Gano about warrantless searches of automobiles. He criticizes the diminished expectation of privacy argument for warrantless searches of automobiles. This argument holds that because people have a diminished expectation of privacy in their automobiles as compared to their homes, the protection against searches should not be as great in automobiles. Gano is concerned this argument may lead to other warrantless searches in public places, such as searches of bags, briefcases, luggage, and the like, pointing out that certainly one has a higher expectation of privacy regarding one's automobile than a paper bag.[1]

Therefore, the answer for Gano is to require warrants for all searches in public places, including automobiles, absent exigent circumstances.[2] The privacy of the individual in public places requires that warrants be issued before searches can be conducted, he argues.

The concern is not the Founding generation's concern about the protection of the individual from government intrusion on his property, but rather the privacy of suspected criminals in public places. Gano also argues that the Supreme Court's decision in *South Dakota v. Opperman* may undermine any standard that prefers warrants when searching automobiles.[3] In *Opperman* the Supreme Court ruled that the police may make routine inventory searches of automobiles within their custody. Gano is concerned that under this rule police can circumvent any requirement for search warrants by impounding the vehicle and then conducting an inventory search. Although the rule is justified as a way of protecting police departments from civil suits, Gano argues that police can already protect themselves from civil suits by closing the windows and locking the doors of automobiles in their custody. For Gano, to permit an inventory search ostensibly to protect the owner when the police suspect they may uncover evidence is disingenuous.[4] The officers are not trying to protect the car owner. Instead, they are really searching for evidence. The police are using the inventory search as an excuse to search for evidence. Therefore, he claims, when police seize a vehicle during a criminal investigation, the inventory exception to the warrant requirement should not be applicable:

> When the police have seized an automobile not in the exercise of some community caretaking function, such as preventing obstruction of highways, but rather pursuant to an investigation of crime, the inventory theory should be inapplicable. Admittedly, it may seem anomalous to protect only those suspected of crime from inventory searches, but unless this is done the inventory search doctrine will render utterly superfluous any rule requiring search warrants. To the extent the anomaly is unacceptable, this should suggest that an inventory search rule of *any* scope might be highly questionable.[5]

According to Gano, if we are to preserve inventory searches of vehicles, therefore, they should only be done on the vehicles of honest citizens, not suspected criminals, meaning that criminals will have more protection than will average citizens. Gano suggests that a way to deal with this inconsistency would be to end warrantless inventory searches, no longer allowing police officers to search vehicles in their custody. One can imagine the civil liabilities of this procedure. The vehicle owner could claim to have had a thousand dollars or the unclaimed winning powerball ticket in the vehicle. Another way to solve the prob-

SEARCHES IN PUBLIC AREAS: EARLY TWENTIETH CENTURY

lem of searching vehicles under the custody of the police would be to say that it is *reasonable* for police officers to conduct inventory searches of *vehicles in their custody*. If items that can clearly be identified as evidence turn up during this search, then under the "plain view" doctrine that evidence would be admissible.[6] Gano's conception of the Fourth Amendment is by no means unique. Indeed, the theme of much twentieth—century jurisprudence has been the expansion of protections for searches in public areas. In this chapter, I will examine the early twentieth century jurisprudence concerning such searches, and in the following chapter I will examine the dramatic change in opinion that began in the 1960's.

The Advent of the Automobile Search: *Carroll v. United States*

Probably the most famous and most often cited case involving search and seizure in a public area is *Carroll v. United States* (1925).[7] *Carroll* is also the first major case involving a search of an automobile. In *Carroll* we see a reaffirmation of the original principle that searches in public areas do not need warrants, although they do need to be reasonable. In this case, George Carroll and John Kiro were convicted of transporting sixty-eight quarts of whiskey and gin in violation of the National Prohibition Act. Carroll and Kiro appealed their conviction, claiming that the search of their automobile that turned up the liquor in question was an unconstitutional search under the Fourth Amendment because the search of the vehicle was conducted without a warrant and that therefore the liquor should be excluded from the trial.[8]

The government's argument that probable cause to search existed in this case is as follows. Federal prohibition agents, working undercover, had met the two defendants at an apartment and agreed to buy three cases of whiskey from the defendants. The defendants were supposed to get the whiskey and bring it back to the apartment, but they never reappeared. The agents noticed, however, that they were driving an Oldsmobile Roadster and wrote down the tag number of the vehicle. About a week later, the same agents were patrolling the road from Detroit to Grand Rapids[9] when they saw the same Oldsmobile—with both Carroll and Kiro in the vehicle—traveling towards Detroit. The agents gave chase but lost the vehicle. A couple of months later, on the same road, the agents passed Carroll and Kiro in the same car going towards Grand Rapids. The agents turned around, followed Carroll and Kiro, and stopped and searched the vehicle. They found behind the upholstering of the seats sixty-eight bottles of whiskey and gin. Carroll and Kiro were arrested.[10]

Chief Justice Taft delivered the Opinion of the Supreme Court,[11] in which he first considered the National Prohibition Act, which was passed to enforce the Eighteenth Amendment. The act makes it unlawful to possess any liquor intended for use in violating the act and provides that no property rights shall exist in such liquor.[12] The act states that no "warrant shall issue to search any private dwelling occupied as such unless it is being used for the unlawful sale of intoxicating liquor, or unless it is in part used for some business purpose such as a store, shop, saloon, restaurant, hotel, or boarding house."[13]

Section 6 of An Act Supplemental to the National Prohibition Act (42. Stat. 222) makes it a misdemeanor punishable by a fine, imprisonment, or both to search any private dwelling without a warrant or to "without a search warrant maliciously and without reasonable cause search any other building or property."[14] In other words, officers cannot search a private dwelling without a search warrant, but can search other buildings without search warrants if the search is not malicious (i. e., without cause).

Since the Court's decision in part turns on its interpretation of the congressional intent in Section Six, it would be helpful to take an in depth look at some of the discussion in Congress over this section. There was a long debate in Congress over Section 6. In arguing against it, some senators emphasized the natural rights basis of the Fourth Amendment. In the words of Senator Reed:

> To my mind it [section 6] involves an invasion of a fundamental principle that is absolutely essential to the maintenance of human liberty. The barbarian, away back in the dim twilight of history, held aloft his shield and brandished his spear, declaring "I am a free man." He had his natural rights as a man—not rights granted to him from a government, but rights that sprang from his Creator . . . . In the course of time their liberties were taken away from them. Then began the struggle to recover them. The barons of Runnymede exacted from King John the cardinal principle from which the fourth amendment to the Constitution was afterwards formulated. Englishmen through the long centuries have proudly held aloft their heads and asserted "the right of castle," the right to walk the streets, "the right to be secure in their persons, their property, their papers, and their effects."[15]

SEARCHES IN PUBLIC AREAS: EARLY TWENTIETH CENTURY

Senator Stanley stated that:

> I have listened to the Senator [Watson] trace those rights back, and they go back to the Scandinavian forests, and then they came from God, and that is what Jefferson meant when he said that they were inalienable. They were not conferred by anybody, they were inherited from God, and all the law can do is to preserve a heritage as divine as life itself and as precious as the soul....[16]

Legislators on both sides of the issue admitted that the legislation allowed warrantless searches of vehicles. In debate on the House floor, Representative Floss asks Representative Volstead, the primary sponsor of the Act (the National Prohibition Act is also known as the Volstead Act), if Section 6 means there will be warrantless searches of vehicles:

> Mr. Floss. Suppose he [the officer] has reason for believing that an automobile which was passing on the road had liquor in it, would he have to have a search warrant in order to search it?
> Mr. Volstead. No; but there is some doubt as to what search he may make. I believe it is section 26 of the prohibition act which provides that an officer may seize an automobile when it is being used for the purpose of carrying liquor. That is because the automobile is forfeited to the United States and because of the familiar doctrine that you may arrest a person in the act of violating the law, and in that connection seize the evidence of his guilt in his immediate possession.[17]

Representative Volstead seems to suggest that the warrantless search is valid when it occurs in conjunction with a valid arrest. But what of a warrantless search based on probable cause? Although he is silent on that, the very first word of his response to the scenario of an officer needing a warrant to search an automobile that he has reason to believe is carrying liquor is "No." That is the scenario of the *Carroll* case.

Another supporter of the act, Representative Mondell, emphasizes that it has been the practice of Congress to allow warrantless searches in some circumstances:

> May I remind the House that at divers times the Congress, in order that there might be no question as to what Congress considered reasonable searches, has in various sections of the Revised Statutes provided for the search of vessels, of vehicles for dutiable articles without warrant, for search of baggage and persons

for concealed dutiable articles without warrant? Congress has provided for the seizure of taxable articles concealed in fraud of the revenue, for search for articles or matters carried in the mail in violation of law, and for search of vehicles transporting liquor into the Indian country.[18]

These laws, Representative Mondell argues, did not cause any outcry over violations of civil liberties:

It is remarkable, it is remarkable that gentlemen have lived all these years with these laws on the statute books and have not become disturbed until the highways of the country have become congested with malefactors, who not only in violation of the Constitution but in violation of State and National law and police regulations insist on bootlegging and rum running.[19]

Senator McKeller further emphasizes the point that the warrant clause should not apply to automobiles:

Amendment 4 of the Constitution was enacted for the purpose of protecting the person and home, and this bill . . . does that . . . . If you apply the principle of the sanctity of the home and of the sanctity of the person to the protection of automobiles, why not apply the same principle to railroad trains and to wagons and to airplanes, and to all other means of transportation?[20]

We see from Senator McKeller's statement that supporters believed the act permitted warrantless searches of automobiles and, as we see in Representative Mondell's comments, argue that this is in keeping with the practice of Congress.

For opponents of the legislation, warrantless searches of vehicles are a problem. According to Representative Graham:

What was the condition when that was written into the Constitution of this free Republic? Was not a man's home his castle? Was not his person free from the unholy touch of any man who dared, under the guise of law or otherwise, to search his person? Yes. If you found a man committing a crime, you might seize him, you might search him, but there was no man in this country that would willingly submit to a search of this person upon the highway without proper authority and the circumstances of the case warranting it. The gentlemen who framed that article [the Fourth Amendment] showed what they thought to be unreasonable by specifically abolishing the general warrant existing at that time.[21]

Congress also discussed whether it would be necessary under the legislation to obtain a warrant to search buildings other than the home. Representative Volstead, in explaining the conference report to the House, states that:

> we absolutely prohibit any search of a dwelling without a warrant, not only under the amendment the House adopted but also under the amendment the conferees have agreed on and now submit. But that did not satisfy the Senate conferees. They insisted that we prevent to some extent the search of other buildings and property. The House conferees refused to go along with that . . .[22]

In other words, the reason for the final wording of Section 6 was that the House conferees insisted that law enforcement officers have the right to search buildings other than homes and other property based on probable cause and without warrants. Indeed, one supporter, Senator Nelson, almost as an aside, states that constitutionally warrants are not even needed to search homes:

> Section 6 . . . is clearly within the pale of the fourth amendment to the Constitution. Indeed, in one respect it is more restrictive, in that it requires a warrant to search a dwelling, a requirement not found in the fourth amendment. As regards all other searches and seizures, it leaves them where the fourth amendment leaves them. They must be reasonable: in other words, based on probable cause as defined by the courts.[23]

Opponents also assumed that warrantless searches would be allowed by the act, and this was one reason for their opposition to the act, as we see in a speech from Senator Stanley:

> It does not matter whether it is a dwelling house, or a storehouse, or a warehouse, or an office; his protection against having his private papers searched, his private property invaded, is just as sacred in one case as in another.[24]

Senator Stanley returns to the original understanding that all premises should be protected by warrants, referring to that original understanding in a passage that I will quote at length:

> The fourth amendment provides that "the right of the people to be secure in their persons, houses"—not dwellings, not homes, but houses—shall not be violated." Did they use the word "houses" meaning "homes?" Was it a loose expression on the part of the makers of the Constitution of the United States? Let us see. It was only a few years before this amendment was written, as I shall further show . . . that the general warrants issued against the citizens of New England, against which James Otis inveighed. . . ., Now, the facts are that these general warrants were not aimed at the homes of the citizens of Boston or anywhere else. These general warrants were used to enter the warehouses of the citizen, to enter their storehouses....[25]

Senator Stanley makes the important observation that the Fourth Amendment says "houses," not "homes," and houses can mean warehouses and storehouses as well as dwelling places, which would seem to be supported by the fact that the general warrants that so inflamed the founding generation were aimed mainly at stores and warehouses (see Chapter 2). Stanley's attempt to amend the act to require warrants for all searches (including those of automobiles) was defeated and the Act Supplemental to the National Prohibition Act was passed with Section 6 intact. As we have seen, Section 6 is intended to allow law enforcement officers to search all but homes without a warrant.

The Supreme Court, in *Carroll*, makes this exact point. It argues that the clear intent of Congress, based on the wording of Section 6, is to require a warrant for the search of a private dwelling, but to require only that a search of other buildings and property be done without malice and with probable cause. Therefore, according to the Court, it is not the intent of Congress to require a warrant to search automobiles for liquor. Automobiles fall under the area of "other property," so only reasonable cause is required.[26]

In this act Congress has lessened the protection of people in buildings other than private dwellings by allowing for warrantless searches. As I have demonstrated, this is in opposition to the Founders' intention to protect people in buildings from warrantless searches. While the Court would appear to acquiesce in Congress's chipping away at the protection afforded us by the Fourth Amendment from warrantless searches on real property, the case involves the search of an automobile, not a store or any other non-dwelling building, and perhaps the Court merely confined itself to the issue at hand. Maybe Taft thought he should rule narrowly, not broadly. Indeed, as we will see in

SEARCHES IN PUBLIC AREAS: EARLY TWENTIETH CENTURY

this section, the Court strongly hints that buildings as well as stores and warehouses enjoy the same protection as dwelling-places.

After looking at a number of recent Fourth Amendment cases and concluding that none concerns the issue in question,[27] Taft, in the Opinion of the Court, turns his attention to the intentions of the framers of that amendment and the early history of the republic after the passage of the amendment:

> On reason and authority the true rule is that if the search and seizure without a warrant are made upon probable cause, that is, upon a belief, reasonably arising out of circumstances known to the seizing officer, that an automobile or other vehicle contains that which by law is subject to seizure and destruction, the search and seizure are valid. *The Fourth Amendment is to be construed in the light of what was deemed an unreasonable search and seizure when it was adopted*, and in a manner which will conserve public interests as well as the interests and rights of individual citizens.[28]

The Court thus holds that the true rule of search and seizure is that an officer does not need a warrant to search a vehicle if the officer reasonably believes he will be able to find items subject to search and seizure. Why do they consider this the true rule? Because, the Court argues, the amendment must be interpreted considering what was deemed a reasonable and unreasonable search at the time of the amendment's adoption, and in a way that protects both the public interest and the rights of individuals. This, it seems, is not far from the Founder's intention to protect natural rights yet also punish wrongdoers. In other words, according to the opinion of the Court, in interpreting the amendment we should go to the intentions and practices of the framers and their generation, and the framers allowed for warrantless searches of vehicles.

In support of its argument, the Court examines one of the laws we discussed in the previous chapter, The Act to Regulate the Collection of Duties, passed by the very same Congress that drafted the Fourth Amendment. The Act required a warrant to search any house, store or building, but allowed for warrantless searches of vessels. The Court points out that like provisions can be found in seven other laws passed between 1790 and 1899.[29] This evidence leads the Court to conclude that:

> the guaranty of freedom from unreasonable searches and seizures

> by the Fourth Amendment has been construed, practically since the beginning of the Government, as recognizing a necessary difference between a search of a *store, dwelling house, or other structure* in respect of which a proper official warrant readily may be obtained, and a search of a ship, motor boat, wagon or automobile, for contraband goods, where it is not practicable to secure a warrant because the vehicle can be quickly moved out of the locality or jurisdiction in which the warrant must be sought.[30]

Thus the Court argues that the history of the country as expressed in its federal laws from the time of the Fourth Amendment supports the contention that the amendment treats searches on real property differently than searches of vehicles. At the same time, the Court also implies that the requirement of search warrants is not limited to dwellings, but extends to stores and other buildings. The Court, therefore, seems to acknowledge, contrary to the congressional intentions expressed in Section 6, that searches of stores and other buildings (i.e., businesses) traditionally have required warrants.[31]

The Court goes on to state that its decision does not mean that officers have the freedom to search anyone for any reason on the highways:

> it would be intolerable and unreasonable if a prohibition agent were authorized to stop every automobile on the chance of finding liquor and thus subject all persons lawfully using the highways to the inconvenience and indignity of such a search.... those... entitled to use the public highways, have a right to free passage without interruption or search unless there is known to a competent official authorized to search, probable cause for believing that their vehicles are carrying contraband or illegal merchandise.[32]

Just because a search warrant is not required to search a vehicle, according to the Court, officers cannot search any vehicle at any time for any reason. They must have probable cause that the vehicles are carrying contraband or illegal merchandise. If officers do not have probable cause the search is not justified and they may be held liable.[33] In other words, the Fourth Amendment protects citizens against unreasonable searches off their property, although it does not require warrants for such searches.

Finally, the Court argues that the search in question was constitutional because probable cause was present. The knowledge the officer

SEARCHES IN PUBLIC AREAS: EARLY TWENTIETH CENTURY

had about the men involved and the men being on a highway that was known as a passageway for bootleggers all added up to probable cause.[34]

The *Carroll* decision has not been universally applauded. One of the leading commentators on the Fourth Amendment, Jacob Landynski, criticizes the decision as being inconsistent with the intentions of the Fourth Amendment. Critical of Taft's presentation of the history of the Fourth Amendment, Landynski argues that there was a better way the Court might have justified its decision:

> *the Court might have made the decision seem more plausible* had it merely stated an exception to the rule that searches and seizures must be authorized by a warrant. The Court might simply have said that the invention of the automobile, with its ability to move contraband goods outside the range of search warrants, made the full requirements of the Fourth Amendment inappropriate for searches of such vehicles. *The amendment was intended principally to protect private dwellings; it need not be construed, in the presence of probable cause, to protect against searches of moving vehicles.*[35]

Landynski argues that the Court could have made its decision more plausible, if still not correct, by creating an exception to the warrant clause. Believing that originally there was no exception to the warrant clause, at least for searches within U.S. borders, he suggests modern circumstances might have justified creating one. His complaint, therefore, is not so much that there cannot be exceptions to the warrant requirement, but rather that if there is going to be an exception, the Court should create it out of whole cloth, if you will, and not rely on misinterpreting history. However, while Landynski states the purpose of the amendment was to protect property, he erroneously limits the protected property to dwelling-houses, forgetting the protection extended to other buildings, like stores and commercial property. Furthermore, as we saw in the previous chapter, there is ample evidence that Americans in previous generations consistently accepted a warrant exception for vehicles; searches in public areas were protected, and they did not require the warrants that searches of property required.

Brinegar v. United States and *United States v. Di Re*: Narrowing the Right to Search in Public Areas

The next major case to involve a vehicle search was *Brinegar v.*

United States.[36] *Brinegar* is important because the Court, while staying with the original understanding concerning searches in public areas, narrows the definition of probable cause and thus makes it easier to contest searches. Brinegar was convicted in a federal district court on the charge of transporting intoxicating liquor into the state of Oklahoma, in violation of the laws of that state.[37] He challenged the conviction because the evidence used against him was liquor seized in a warrantless search of his car. He argued that this warrantless search violated the Fourth Amendment. Under the exclusionary rule, he wanted the evidence quashed and the conviction overturned. The Supreme Court disagreed and upheld the conviction.[38]

In their written opinion, the Court does not really consider the question of whether it is constitutional under the Fourth Amendment to search a vehicle without a warrant. Using *Carroll* as its guide, it merely assumes that it is. The Court is careful to repeat the *Carroll* Court's dictum that this does not mean that officers can search any vehicle for any reason, emphasizing that the officers must have probable cause to search. Thus, their argument centers on whether the officers had probable cause to search.[39]

In a footnote, the Court quotes John Marshall's famous definition of probable cause in *Locke v. United States*—circumstances that warrant suspicion—to argue that modern judges require more than suspicion. Quoting *Carroll*, the Court states that probable cause means:

> the facts and circumstances within their [the officers] knowledge and of which they had reasonably trustworthy information [are] sufficient in themselves to warrant a man of reasonable caution in the belief that' an offense has been or is being committed.[40]

In other words, a reasonable person, given the facts and circumstances, not only has to suspect but to believe that an offense has been or will be committed. Mere suspicion is not enough. The officer must actually believe that a crime has or will be committed. Belief requires a higher standard of certainty. In this aspect of the decision, the Court narrows the original understanding of probable cause, broadening the protections of suspects in public areas.

Justice Jackson wrote the dissenting opinion in the case, joined by Justices Frankfurter and Murphy. Jackson's dissent is very important because he would narrow the standard for warrantless searches in public areas even further. He argues that all warrantless searches are illegal

SEARCHES IN PUBLIC AREAS: EARLY TWENTIETH CENTURY

unless authorized by congressional legislation. All three of the dissenting judges were among the New Deal justices (as was Frankfurter and Murphy) who revolutionized constitutional law.[41] For them, what differentiates *Brinegar* from *Carroll* is that in *Carroll* the warrantless search was authorized by congressional legislation, allowing officers to conduct warrantless searches of vehicles illegally transporting liquor. Jackson argues that the Court's allowing the warrantless search in *Carroll* was an act of judicial restraint, for to strike down the warrantless search they would have had to strike down the congressional law that authorized the search. Instead, they deferred to the legislature and allowed the warrantless search as consistent with the Fourth Amendment. Without that congressional authorization, Jackson clearly believes, the search would have been illegal.

The thoughts expressed by Jackson in the dissenting opinion in *Brinegar* were based on the Opinion of the Supreme Court he wrote in the case of *United States v. Di Re*,[42] which restricted the ability of officers to search in public areas. In *Di Re* government agents were told by an informer that someone was going to sell the informer counterfeit gasoline coupons. Appearing at the arranged selling place, the government agents found the suspect, the informer, and a third person (Di Re) in a car transacting the sale of the coupons. The agents took all three into custody and searched. The agents found more counterfeit coupons in Di Re's pockets and he was later *convicted* in federal court. The Supreme Court overturned Di Re's conviction. The Court said two questions had to be considered. First, did the officers have the right to conduct a warrantless search of an automobile based on probable cause that it contained contraband? Jackson answered this question negatively. He said *Carroll* was not a precedent because *Carroll* involved a congressional authorization to conduct warrantless automobile searches, while this case did not involve a congressional authorization. The courts could not allow a warrantless search, Jackson argued, unless Congress had specifically authorized a warrantless search (as was the case in *Carroll*). Absent congressional authorization, warrantless searches were unconstitutional. Jackson does not say why a warrantless search conducted under congressional approval is constitutional, while one conducted without congressional approval is not. If warrantless searches are unconstitutional, one might ask what right does Congress have to violate the constitution? Secondly, even if *Carroll* could be read broadly to allow for warrantless searches of cars without congressional authorization, the search in the current case was still illegal because an authorization to search a vehicle does not give an officer the right to search any passenger who happens to be in the vehicle. Just as having a search warrant to search a house does not give the officer the right to search every person in the house, so, too, the right to search a car does not give the officer the right to search every person in the car. The officer must have probable cause to search the person. In this case, because Di Re, although in the car, was not involved in the illegal transaction, there was no probable cause to search him.

Although some commentators applaud Jackson's opinion as an attempt to limit the effects of the *Carroll* case,[43] its claim that prior legislative approval is needed before warrantless searches can be considered legitimate is not borne out by history. As we saw in the previous chapter, the early generations considered warrantless searches and seizures not authorized by statute, conducted outside of real property, constitutional.[44] As to Jackson's second point, as we saw in Chapter 3, the original standard was that probable cause justified a warrantless search in public areas. One's natural rights did not include the right to do wrong. The Founders wanted to protect the public from criminals.

One way of doing that was to allow warrantless searches in public areas if there was probable cause. By not allowing such searches, suspected criminals could escape punishment (it being impracticable to stop the suspect, go to a judge and get a warrant, then go back and search the suspect). Being in a car while the obvious transaction of a felony is taking place in that car would seem to be *probable* cause, leaving Jackson's reasoning subject to criticism on both points. It is Jackson's reasoning, however, that the Court will adopt in the 1960s, as we shall see in the next chapter.

Conclusion

In the cases presented in this chapter, particularly *Brinegar* and *Di Re*, we begin to see a weakening of the original understanding concerning searches in public areas. The majority of the Court in *Di Re*, and a minority in *Brinegar*, begin the process of strengthening the protections for people in public areas, by narrowing the probable cause standard, and rejecting the notion that warrantless searches, without congressional authorization, are constitutional. Thus judges and other public officials begin to move their concern from that of property owners to suspected criminal officials. Since judges and other public officials become more concerned with the rights of suspected criminals, their concern sifts from searches of private property to searches in public areas. In so doing, they make it harder to convict criminals for crimes they have committed. These are perhaps only small steps, but steps they are along the way toward a complete rejection of the original standard concerning searches in public areas that is accomplished in the 1960's and 70's.

CHAPTER 5

SEARCHES IN PUBLIC AREAS: THE LATE TWENTIETH CENTURY

I explained in the last chapter that in the mid twentieth century there begins a movement away from the original understanding of the Fourth Amendment. The original understanding of the Fourth Amendment - that searches in public areas could be conducted without warrants – was replaced with a standard that affords greater protection to suspected criminals in public areas (i.e., roads, sidewalks, public buildings) and less protection for private property. This movement increased dramatically in the 1970's. Justice Jackson's interpretation of the amendment in *Brinegar* and *Di Re* wins the day. This change occurs as a result of a change in the conception of justice. Many modern judges adopt a radical individualistic conception of rights where rights are divorced from morality and freedom becomes license to do what one wants, as long as no one else is harmed. In addition, as I will discuss in the conclusion, during this period, criminals come to be seen as the victims of society, instead of the vexation—at least among some opinion leaders. So when it comes to the Fourth Amendment, and many other areas of criminal law, the emphasis of the courts, and many opinion leaders, shifts to protecting the rights of criminals. In search and seizure law, this means, as I will show, making it more difficult for officers to conduct searches in public areas.

Chadwick: Requiring Warrants to Search in Public Areas

In *United States v. Chadwick*[1] the Supreme Court ruled unconstitutional the warrantless search of a footlocker based on a "hit" from a drug-sniffing dog. Federal narcotic agents had acted on a tip that two people arriving in Boston on a train from San Diego might be carrying drugs. The two people, one of whom matched the profile used to spot drug traffickers, were carrying a footlocker that was heavy for its size and leaking talcum powder, a substance commonly used to mask the odor of marijuana or hashish.[2] The officers watched the two suspects as they carried the footlocker for a short distance and then sat down, at which point the officers released a drug-sniffing dog who signaled the presence of a controlled substance in the footlocker. The suspects then met a third man, Chadwick, and all three people took the footlocker to Chadwick's car and placed it in the trunk. The officers arrested all three individuals and took the car containing the footlocker to the federal building in Boston. The footlocker was placed in an evidence room at the federal building and later opened by the officers, who found a large amount of marijuana inside.[3]

During the trial in district court, the federal government justified the warrantless search by citing the automobile exception and search—incident—to-arrest exceptions to the warrant clause of the Fourth Amendment. Under the automobile exception, as we saw in *Carroll*, vehicles could be searched without a warrant, if there was probable cause for doing so. The search-incident-to-arrest exception allows law enforcement officers to search, without a warrant: (1) the person being arrested; and (2) anything in the "immediate control" of the person being arrested from which he may gain possession of evidence or a weapon.[4] The district court rejected both arguments, saying neither justified the search. The court said that the relationship between the footlocker and Chadwick's automobile was merely coincidental (the officers could have stopped the men and searched the footlocker at the train station, and it was the footlocker, not the car, that was the object of the search) and so the automobile exception did not apply. As for the search-incident-to-arrest exception, the court ruled that the footlocker was not part of the area from which Chadwick and friends could gain possession of a weapon or destructible evidence.

The court of appeals upheld the federal district court's decision, although it noted that the officers did have probable cause to believe that the footlocker contained a controlled substance. The question, then, for the court of appeals was not whether there was probable cause, but whether probable cause is enough to permit a search in this instance. The government in arguing its case had claimed that movable personality (personal property) lawfully seized in a public place should be subject to search without a warrant if probable cause exists that it contains evidence of a crime. While "such personality shares some characteristics of mobility which supports automobile searches, the court [of appeals] nevertheless concluded that a rule permitting a search of personality on probable cause alone had not yet 'received sufficient recognition by the Supreme Court outside the automobile area . . . for it to be recognized as a valid exception to the Fourth Amendment warrant requirement.'"[5] So, the court rejected the government's point that movable personal property could be searched in public areas without a warrant. The general rule is that a warrant is required for searches. The Supreme Court has created an exception for automobiles, allowing warrantless searches. But it has not created an exception for movable personal property. So the general rule stands and a warrantless search of personal property is a violation of the Fourth Amendment.

When the case came before the Supreme Court, the federal government argued that the warrant requirement only protects homes, offices and private communications. "In all other situations . . . less significant privacy values are at stake, and the reasonableness of a government intrusion should depend solely on whether there is probable cause...."[6] The Supreme Court, quoting a famous dictum from *Katz* that the Fourth Amendment "protects people not places," rejected the government's argument.[7] Warrantless searches in public places were not condemned at the time of the Founding because such searches were not an important issue in colonial America, the Court argued. So, in other words, the original Fourth Amendment has nothing to say about searches in public areas because the framers of the Amendment were not even thinking about such searches. It is not that the Fourth Amendment allows warrantless searches in public areas, rather, it is silent concerning such searches. Therefore, the implication is, modern judges are free to set up their own rules, based on modern circumstances, concerning public searches. (As I have discussed previously, however, warrantless searches in public areas did take place.) What the Founders did intend, the Court said, was to protect fundamental values, and the fundamental value of safety from unreasonable searches and seizures is best protected through judicial warrant. In common with modern judges and legal scholars, the Court seems to argue that it is following the spirit of the Constitution while adjusting to the reality of modern circumstances. Times change and we face things—like warrantless searches in public places—that the Founders did not dream of.[8] In this case, the judges decide that only certain narrowly defined exceptions to the warrant clause are appropriate. Movable personal property, such as the footlocker, does not fall under any of these exceptions. Accordingly, the warrantless search of the footlocker is unconstitutional.[9]

The difference between this case and a car search case like *Brinegar*, according to the Supreme Court, is that there is a diminished expectation of privacy in automobiles, but not in luggage. Quoting *Cardwell v. Lewis*,[10] the Court says, "'One has a lesser expectation of privacy in a motor vehicle because its function is transportation and it seldom serves as one's residence or as the repository of personal effects. It travels public thoroughfares where both its occupants and its contents are in plain view.'"[11]

Furthermore, the Court argues, automobiles are subject to state registration and inspection requirements that also lessen the expectation of privacy. Luggage contents, in contrast, are not open to public view, except as a condition of border entry or common carrier travel. Luggage is intended as a repository of personal effects. Therefore "a person's expectations of privacy in personal luggage are substantially greater than in an automobile."[12] So, to protect those greater privacy rights a warrant is necessary to search luggage. Unlike automobile searches, probable cause will not be enough to justify such searches.

Justice Blackmun writes a dissent in this case in which Justice Rehnquist joins. Interestingly, Blackmun begins his dissent by condemning the government's argument (and the argument of this study) that the warrant requirement should be limited to structures. He calls this argument "unfortunate," "extreme" and "overbroad." Blackmun argues that it would be better to adopt a policy of allowing a warrantless search of any property seized in conjunction with a valid arrest in a public place. He argues that the Court is letting circumstances determine the outcome of the case. Blackmun contends that if the arrest had been committed earlier, that is, after the two suspects had gotten off the train and were sitting on the footlocker, the warrantless search of the footlocker would have been constitutional under the search—incident—to-arrest exception to the warrant requirement that allows searches of items within the immediate grasp of the suspect. Citing a number of courts of appeals cases, Blackmun argued that the suspects' "immediate control" would include luggage and briefcases.[13] Alternatively, if the agents had waited longer and arrested the individuals as they drove off in the car, the warrantless search of the footlocker would have been constitutional under the automobile exception to the warrant clause.[14] A search a few minutes earlier or a few minutes later would have been constitutional, but a search of the footlocker at the federal building is unconstitutional.

Blackmun's complaint is that the Court, by being so technical, is confusing law enforcement officers. When can they search, and when can they not search? Blackmun is right in one respect. The Court would be better off adopting one clear principle. His principle, however, is wrong. Blackmun, like the rest of the Court, ignores the principle of the Fourth Amendment that differentiates between searches in public areas and searches on property. It is not just that a warrantless search incident to arrest in a public place may be conducted on probable cause, but all searches in public places based on probable cause are constitutional. Use of the original standard would have resolved this case more clearly. Since there was probable cause (as the court of appeals acknowledged) and since the search was in a public place, it should be constitutional. The same goes for searches incident to arrest, automobile searches, searches of packages, etc. As long as probable cause is established the search is constitutional.

It should be pointed out, however, that Justice Brennan, in his concurring opinion, argues that Blackmun misinterprets some of his evidence. Brennan notes that it was not the Supreme Court, but rather courts of appeals decisions, that are cited by Blackmun to suggest that the search of the footlocker would be constitutional either under the automobile or the search—incident—to-arrest exceptions to the warrant requirement. So Brennan states that it is not at all clear to him that the contents of locked containers can be searched under the automobile exception, or that a secured footlocker can be searched as part of the search—incident—to—arrest exception. The Court will attempt to clarify this in future cases.

What is clear is that this decision is a complete victory for the modern interpretation of the Fourth Amendment. The Court bends over backwards to protect certain forms of privacy—the privacy of drug dealers and users in their cars, luggage and persons. At the same time it refuses to take up the argument that the amendment's purpose was to protect people from unwarranted government intrusion on their property, and so denigrates the privacy of people like businessmen. The Court's interest has moved from protecting the rights of property holders to protecting the privacy rights of suspected criminals.

Ross and Sanders and Searches of Packages in Cars

The next important car search case was *Arkansas v. Sanders*.[15] In *Sanders*, the Court expanded the privacy standard for Fourth Amendment protections by arguing that containers within cars were protected from warrantless searches, because of the expectation of privacy. Arkansas police had probable cause to suspect that a suitcase contained marijuana. They watched as the defendant placed the suitcase in the trunk of a taxi and drove away. The police pursued the taxi for several blocks, then stopped it, opened the trunk, and searched the suitcase without a warrant.[16] The Court disallowed the search. Although the suitcase was found in the car, the Court ruled that the search was not covered by the automobile exception to the warrant clause. Since the suspected illegal substances were in the suitcase, which the officers saw before it was put into the car, there was probable cause to search only the luggage, not the car itself.[17] After *Chadwick*, luggage in a vehicle had higher protection under the Fourth Amendment, and therefore officers needed a warrant to search the luggage.

Here we reach what one commentator has called the Fourth Amendment tarbaby.[18] After *Chadwick* and *Sanders,* if there is probable cause to search a car the car may be searched—including, by the way, locked compartments in the car (that is, the glove compartment and trunk) -- without a warrant. However, officers cannot search a container in a car, for example, luggage and briefcases. The only standard is that the Supreme Court has determined that there is more of an expectation of privacy in luggage, briefcases and other closed containers, than in a car. Some car searches will require warrants and some will not. The Court, in its effort to clarify the rules concerning car searches, has simply created uncertainty.

In defense of the *Sanders* Court its ruling avoids a situation in which officers purposely wait for a suspect to put luggage in a car so that they may search the luggage without a warrant as allowed by the automobile exception (as happened in *Chadwick*). A better way of solving the problem would have been to return to the original understanding of the Fourth Amendment and dispose of the warrant requirement for luggage. Officers would then have no reason to wait for the suspect to drive off in a car (and maybe drive away). If there is probable cause to search the luggage, whether the luggage is in a car or with a person on a public street, the officer should have the right to search it. Had the Court so ruled in *Chadwick*, *Sanders* would have been unnecessary. One could say that *Sanders* is an example of bad constitutional law making more work for the Supreme Court. The Court bases its decision on "the expectation of privacy." Then it has to decide on a case by case basis whether the particular situation (car searches, luggage searches, luggage in car searches) involves a privacy interest that may require a warrant. And by splitting hairs—by saying car searches do not require warrants, but luggage searches do—the Court is simply inviting new litigation when different situations crop up ("ok, what about luggage in cars"?). The original standard was much simpler. If the search was in a public area, be it an automobile search, or a search of a briefcase, it required probable cause but not a warrant.

Three years later the Court tries to clarify car search rules in *United States v. Ross*.[19] In this case the Court ruled that police officers who had probable cause to search an automobile may do so without a warrant. This is in keeping with *Carroll*. The Court went on to say that this power to search without a warrant included the right to search containers in the automobile, including locked suitcases, but only when the police officer had probable cause to search the whole car. If the officer had probable cause to search only a particular container in the car, then the *Chadwick-Sanders* rule applied and the officer must have a warrant to search the container. So the procedure depends on whether or not the officer has cause to search the entire car, or only a container in the car.

In *Ross* an informant told police that he had seen Ross complete a drug deal using drugs he had stored in the trunk of his car. The police stopped the car, searched it, and found the drugs in a paper bag in the trunk of the car. The Court ruled that since all the officers knew was that Ross sold the drugs out of the trunk of his car; they had probable cause to search the car and any closed containers found in it. If the police had known specifically that the drugs were in a closed brown paper bag, then the *Chadwick* rule would have applied and a warrant would have been needed to search the bag:

> The scope of a warrantless search based on probable cause is no narrower—and no broader—than the scope of a search authorized by a warrant supported by probable cause.... If probable cause justifies the search of a lawfully stopped vehicle, it justifies the search of every part of the vehicle and its contents that may conceal the object of the search.[20]

Examine for a moment the status of car searches after *Ross*. Under the *Carroll* rule, as expanded in *Ross*, law enforcement officers may conduct a warrantless search of a car, including both closed compartments and closed containers in it, if there is probable cause to search the car. Under *Chadwick-Sanders*, however, if police stop a car and they have probable cause to suspect that a certain container in the car holds evidence, the officers must first obtain a warrant to search the container. Similar situations arise in both cases—the officer stops a car and has reason to suspect it contains illegal goods. In one case he suspects that the goods are somewhere in the car (that is, the liquor smuggling in *Carroll*). He may legally search the entire car, including closed compartments and closed containers, without a warrant and seize any illegal goods he finds as evidence to be used in court. In the second case, the officer stops a car and has probable cause to suspect that a specific container holds illegal goods (drugs in luggage as in *Sanders*). Here, if the officer searches without a warrant, the evidence he seizes is excluded from court and the suspect will probably go free for lack of evidence. As a result of *Ross* when an officer stops a car, before he searches he has to decide if he has probable cause to search the whole car or just a container in the car. The officer may have to make a split-second decision, one that could affect the prosecutor's ability to prove a suspect's guilt.

Acevedo—A Return to the Original Understanding?

Recently, the Court has seemed to return to the original understanding of the Fourth Amendment—at least when it comes to car searches. A good example of this is *California v. Acevedo*.[21] Police observed Acevedo leave an apartment known to contain marijuana. He was carrying a paper bag the size of marijuana bags the officers had seen earlier. Acevedo placed the bag in the trunk of his car and then drove off. The police stopped the car, searched the trunk, and opened the bag – to find marijuana. Acevedo's motion to suppress the marijuana as evidence was denied and he pled guilty to possession of marijuana for sale.

The California Court of Appeals held that the marijuana should have been suppressed as evidence. It held that this case was controlled by *Chadwick*, because though the officers had probable cause to believe the bag contained marijuana they did not have probable cause to believe that the car itself otherwise contained contraband.

Given that lower courts are supposed to comply with Supreme Court precedent and given the Supreme Court precedent in the *Chadwick-Sanders-Ross* line of cases, it is hard to argue with the California Court of Appeal's decision. Obviously the probable cause involved the bag, not the entire car. In another example of the Court's confusing topsy-turvy Fourth Amendment jurisprudence, the Supreme Court overruled the California Court of Criminal Appeals, stating that the evidence gained from the search was admissible. The Court held that the police, in a search that included only a container in a car, may search the container without a warrant if there is probable cause.[22] *Carroll v. United States*, the court said, controls all car searches,[23] and *Carroll* required only probable cause, not a search warrant. The Court ruled that *stare decisis* did not prevent it from overturning the *Chadwick-Sanders* rule governing the search of packages in vehicles when there was probable cause to search only the package.[24] The Court argues that the *Chadwick-Sanders* rule provides only minimal protection since police, knowing they can search closed containers if they are searching the entire car, may search more extensively than they otherwise might in order to establish probable cause to search the car.[25] Furthermore, the *Chadwick-Sanders* rule is the opposite of a clear and unequivocal guideline and thus has confused the courts and police officers and impeded effective law enforcement.[26] The Court emphasizes that its decision is not an expansion of the *Carroll* doctrine. For example, in this case the officers may search the bag without a warrant, but since they have probable cause to search only the bag then that is all they can search. The right to search the bag does not give them the right to search the rest of the car.[27] In this case since the officers saw Acevedo place the bag in the trunk, they had probable cause to search only the bag, not the rest of the car.[28] The opinion of the Court ends with this statement:

> Until today, this Court has drawn a curious line between the search of an automobile that coincidentally turns up a container and the search of a container that coincidentally turns up in an automobile. The protections of the Fourth Amendment must not turn on such coincidences. We therefore interpret *Carroll* as providing one rule to govern all automobile searches. The police may search an automobile and the containers within it where they have probable cause to believe contraband or evidence is contained.[29]

This decision resolves a confusing interpretation of the Fourth Amendment by returning to its original understanding. In all searches involving automobiles the standard will be the original standard of probable cause, not the warrant requirement the Court invented in *Chadwick-Sanders*. In the realm of automobile searches, this decision corrected much Court-imposed mischief.

Could the Court have gone further? One of the more important aspects of this decision is Justice Scalia's concurring opinion, in which he points out the inconsistent nature of the Court's Fourth Amendment jurisprudence when it comes to searches in public areas:

> I agree with the dissent [written by Justice Stevens and joined in by Justices White and Marshall] that it is anomalous for a briefcase to be protected by the "general requirement" of a prior warrant when it is being carried along the street, but for that same briefcase to become unprotected as soon as it is carried into an automobile. On the other hand, I agree with the Court that it would be anomalous for a locked compartment in an automobile to be unprotected by the "general requirement" of a prior warrant, but for an unlocked briefcase within the automobile to be protected. I join in the judgment of the Court because I think its holding is more faithful to the text and tradition of the Fourth Amendment, and if these anomalies in our jurisprudence are ever to be eliminated that is the direction in which we should travel.[30]

Scalia points out that although the Court has resolved the confusion surrounding its car search jurisprudence with this decision, confusion enough remains in Fourth Amendment jurisprudence generally. This confusing jurisprudence creates situations such as the one described above, in which a briefcase being carried down a street is covered by the warrant requirement, while a briefcase being carried in a car is not. The solution to this problem, for Scalia, is to return to the Founding generation's understanding of the Fourth Amendment.

According to Scalia, the modern Supreme Court has gone back and forth between imposing a categorical warrant requirement and looking to reasonableness alone. In the 1960s the preference for a warrant won out, at least rhetorically. Scalia explains that the victory was illusory, since there are some twenty exceptions to the warrant requirement.[31] *Acevedo* does not represent a departure from modern Fourth Amendment jurisprudence, but is merely another example of the Court's inconsistent jurisprudence.[32]

Scalia would return "to the first principle that the 'reasonableness' requirement of the Fourth Amendment affords the protection that the common law afforded," meaning that warrants should be required where the common law required them. Scalia adds that "the supposed 'general rule' that a warrant is always required does not appear to have any basis in common law."[33]

What is this common law standard? Scalia does not quite say. However, he gives a hint in the final paragraph of his opinion:

> I would reverse the judgment in the present case, not because a closed container carried inside a car becomes subject to the "automobile exception" to the general warrant requirement, but because the search of a closed container, *outside a privately owned building*, with probable cause to believe that the container contains contraband, and when it in fact does contain contraband, is not one of those searches whose Fourth Amendment reasonableness depends upon a warrant. For that reason I concur in the judgment of the Court.[34]

As I demonstrated in Chapter 1, this is the old common law standard. Searches on private premises generally required warrants, while searches in public areas generally did not. Here Justice Scalia, by specifying the location of the search as "outside a privately owned building," refers to this common law differentiation between searches on private property and searches in public areas. The modern Court, as we have seen, has attempted to collapse this distinction, but then creates confusion by allowing all types of exceptions to the warrant requirement.

Scalia does discuss the Supreme Court's near complete abandonment of the original understanding of the Fourth Amendment. For while the Court has tightened the requirements for searches off private property, it has loosened the requirements for searches on some types of private property, mainly in private businesses. The Court doubly rejects the original understanding. By expanding the protection (at least for a while) in public areas, and diminishing the protection on property, the Court turns the Fourth Amendment on its head. To understand this further, in the next chapter I will look at the modern Supreme Court's interpretation of the Fourth Amendment protection of private businesses.

Conclusion: *Memoirs v. Massachusetts* and the Modern Conception of Justice

I have shown that the judiciary in the twentieth century creates more and more protections for people in public areas. The traditional belief that searches in public areas require probable cause is replaced (at least until some rethinking in *Acevedo* and *Ross*) with the belief that these searches require warrants. As I mentioned earlier, one reason for this reversal is a change in the conception of justice. The modern idea of justice replaces the Founders' idea in which liberty was not confused with license. The Founders believed "self government" referred to governing one's passions as well as to a democratic system of government.

In fact, they believed liberty required this first type of self-government.

The trend in the twentieth century has been to confuse liberty with license. Activities that were traditionally considered immoral, such as drug use and pornography, are considered simple matters of taste, neither moral nor immoral, but an expression of personal preference. This view may be best exemplified by Justice Douglas's concurring opinion in the 1966 Supreme Court case of *Memoirs v. Massachusetts*.[35] Here the Supreme Court overturned Massachusetts state court decisions holding the novel *Fanny Hill* obscene, because the book "has at least 'some minimal literary value.'"[36] Justice Douglas argues that the Massachusetts state court opinion is wrong because "censorship of expression not brigaded with illegal action" is wrong and violates the First Amendment.[37] In other words, obscene speech should be protected. There is no standard of right and wrong when it comes to expression. As long as the expression does not promote illegal action, it should be allowed. Indeed, far from being harmful, pornography may have beneficial effects, according to Douglas:

> Perhaps the most frequently assigned justification for censorship is the belief that erotica produce antisocial sexual conduct. But that relationship has yet to be proven. Indeed, if one were to make judgments on the basis of speculation, one might guess that literature of the most pornographic sort would, in many cases, provide substitute—not a stimulus—for antisocial conduct. As I read the First Amendment, judges cannot gear the literary diet of an entire nation to whatever tepid stuff is incapable of triggering the most demented mind. The First Amendment demands more than a horrible example or two of the perpetrator of a crime of sexual violence, in whose pocket is found a pornographic book, before it allows the Nation to be saddled with a regime of censorship.[38]

What had traditionally been considered an evil, pornography, might actually be a social good, in Douglas' view. Instead of leading to sexual violence, it might actually alleviate it. Instead of being evil, pornography is just a matter of taste ("literary diet").

We see here the modern tendency, including the modern judiciary's tendency, to consider neutral – or even good—activity that was previously considered wrong. There is no natural standard of justice –

no natural law. We have no natural rights. All is a matter of taste or preference. This may be one reason why twentieth-century judges have become more concerned with searches in public areas. Many of the searches discussed in the last two chapters involved alcohol or drugs, activities that many modern elites do not consider wrong but rather a matter of personal preference.[39] By making searches in public areas harder to conduct, the courts protect activities that had traditionally been considered immoral. The right to privacy becomes the right to do wrong.

CHAPTER 6
THE NEW DEAL AND COMMERCIAL SEARCHES

The alteration from the Founders' approach to searches in public areas that I demonstrated in the last two chapters is not the only movement in twentieth-century Fourth Amendment jurisprudence. There is also a radical change in the judiciary's approach to search of commercial property. But whereas the twentieth century saw increased protections for searches in public areas, when it comes to commercial searches protection declines. The New Deal brought into being a large administrative state, which was accompanied by a corresponding expansion of the state's power to search commercial property. This is not coincidental: as the duties of government expand, the methods used by government to carry out those duties likewise expand. The Fourth Amendment rights of businessmen become an offering paid to the altar of the administrative state. Commenting on only one area of the government's responsibilities, worker safety, Carlos Castillo describes this development:

> The twentieth century has witnessed a steady increase in governmental regulatory activity, especially in the commercial context. As a result of the eagerness of federal and state governments to promote the safety of workers, businesses are constantly under the watchful eye of governmental agencies. In carrying out their duties, agencies quite often presume the ability to enter and inspect a business' premises and operations. . . . During such inspections, governmental investigative power frequently clashes with employers' fourth amendment rights against unreasonable searches and

seizures.¹

The businessman usually loses this clash.

In further contrast to its stance on vehicle searches, the modern judiciary has ruled fairly consistently on searches of private dwellings. Modern judges agree with Silas Wasserstrom and Louis Seidman, who have noted that the Fourth Amendment requirement "that no warrants be issued without probable cause is a powerful structural reason for insisting that at least some searches and seizures be preceded by warrants."² Most modern judges have held that except in emergency circumstances, searches of private dwellings require search warrants. In this area the Court has been consistent with the original intentions of the Fourth Amendment Framers.³ As Nelson Lasson has remarked, according to Supreme Court jurisprudence:

> The only circumstance which allows entry and search of a dwelling without a warrant is that in which the officer witnesses the commission of an offense inside the house and therefore has the right to enter for the purpose of making the arrest...searches of dwellings without a valid warrant are otherwise unlawful, notwithstanding facts unquestionably showing probable cause.⁴

Lasson adds, "this rule (requiring warrants) has been held to apply to offices also."⁵ Unfortunately, this last statement, while basically true in 1937 when Lasson wrote *History and Development*, is no longer correct. When it comes to searches of commercial property, the story is now very different.

The Rise of the New Deal and the Rise of the Administrative Search

The success of Progressive and New Deal ideas is seen in the 1940's, when a dramatic change in Fourth Amendment jurisprudence occurs. The Court and Congress allow the government much more freedom than in previous decades in executing searches on commercial property, by permitting warrantless searches therein. Two leading commercial Fourth Amendment cases of this decade—*Oklahoma Press Publishing Co. v. Walling* and *Davis v. United States* – establish precedents for warrantless searches on commercial property.

In *Oklahoma Press Publishing Co. v. Walling* (1946),⁶ an administrator for the Wage and Hour Division of the U.S. Department of Labor sought judicial enforcement of a subpoena requiring the Oklahoma Press Publishing Company to turn over certain records pursuant to Sections 9 and 11(a) of the Fair Labor Standards Act.[7]

Section 9 of the Act gives the federal administrators the authority to subpoena information from companies. Section 11(a) authorizes the administrator to:

> enter and inspect such places and such records (and make such transcriptions thereof), question such employees, and investigate such facts, conditions, practices, or matters as he may deem necessary or appropriate to determine whether any person has violated any provision of this Act, or which may aid in the enforcement of the provisions of this Act.[8]

The supporters of the Fair Labor Standards Act argued that it was needed to alleviate the condition of the poor, and that it advanced the cause of political freedom. Representative Dorsey, speaking in support of the Act, glorified it in these terms:

> Step by step this world is getting more reasonable despite the chaos we see in many places. We can trace the trend from the Magna Carta, through our separation from the mother country, and up to this very Wagner Labor Relations Act and wage and hour legislation . . . . We find the pathway strewn with reactionaries and obstructionists. Every improvement has produced its crop of opponents who fought progress or suggested that we should do our reforming tomorrow instead of today. It is the story of the winning of our political freedom.[9]

Senator Schwellenbach went even further, to suggest a direct link between the Act and political freedom:

> down through the ages mankind has sought two goals. One of them has been political security. . . . the reason why men have sought political liberties, why they have sought the right to freedom of religion, why they have sought the right to freedom of the press was not for the purpose of securing those rights in themselves . . . .When the original patriarchal or matriarchal tribes were formed, the individuals who agreed to the formation of those tribes gave up some of their liberties.
> . . .They were willing to give up their absolute freedom because of the fact the tribe would protect them from some poacher.
> . . .The goal of economic security is and always has

been the goal which mankind has sought.[10]

According to Senator Schwellenbach, economic security is more important than liberty. Political liberty serves the purpose of ensuring economic security. And the Fair Labor Standards Act, in his view, provided economic security for the great number of Americans through the establishment of a minimum wage and other standards.

One might contrast this view to that of the Founders, who were also concerned with economics, in particular with protecting the right to acquire and keep property. The Founders believed, as I discussed in Chapter Three, that man had a natural right to property, to the profit made possible by the sweat of his brow. Furthermore, private property was considered important because it protected man's freedoms. This right is a necessary condition of liberty, helping to check the power of government. According to the Founders it is the existence of private property that secures liberty. For the Founders economics is in service of the political. One purpose of a free economy and property rights is to protect man's political liberty.

Some congressmen were opposed to the Fair Labor Standards Act because of a concern for liberty. In remarks that are particularly pertinent for this study, Representative Dondero raises the specter of unreasonable searches and seizures:

> If this bill becomes law, the private affairs of the employer of labor in this country will become the property of a board of politically appointed snoopers. The private records of all business will be open to investigation. Search and seizure will be common. No employer will be safe from the prying eyes of his competitors. An employer would not be permitted to discharge the fomenters of trouble in his own establishment without asking Washington.[11]

Representative Cox of Georgia made a similar point:

> The administration of the act would call for an army of snoopers, inspectors, counselors, and other agents, particularly susceptible to partisan abuses and political manipulations, and would throw all business and industry into the political field.
>
> Both employers and employees would do well to remember that Federal control is a two-edged sword that cuts both ways. The powers so vested in Federal authority could as easily be used by a government hostile to free industry to crush it, as it could be used by a government hostile to labor to enslave it.[12]

Representatives Dondero and Cox objected to the Fair Labor Standards Act not only because they believed it would lead to widespread search and seizure of employers' records. They thought it would poke a hole in that "great fence of liberty," by making business and labor that much more dependent on, and subservient to, the federal government. They subscribe to the old saying that a government that is big enough to help you is big enough to hurt you.

Congressmen Michener sums up concerns on the legislation in his comments about Section 9, one of the sections involved in *Oklahoma Press Publishing Company v. Walling*. His comments deserve to be quoted at length:

> ... section 9 is of special interest because this is one of the "snooping" sections of the bill. Imagine the feeling of the merchant or the industry up in your district when a "designated representative" presents himself in the office and demands the right to make an investigation and "gather data regarding the wages, hours, and other conditions and practices of employment in the industry." Yet the bill goes further and provides that this representative of Madam Perkins [FDR's Secretary of Labor] may "enter and inspect such places and such records." Yes; and that is not all; and here the ultimate is reached. I know of no previous law going quite so far, because this bill provides that this "investigator" may "make such transcripts thereof" – having reference to the books and records of the industry – as this "investigator" may deem advisable. Has the time come when a representative of a bureaucrat in Washington may brazenly enter the business offices of all industry throughout the country and, for reasons best known to himself or the Secretary of Labor, take away with him "transcripts" and copies of the records kept in the offices of these private business institutions? ... Bureaucratic tyranny is intolerable.[13]

Representative Michener, in his statement, returns to the Founders' understanding of search and seizure. The government should only trespass on private property, including commercial property, if there is probable cause that wrongdoing has occurred. The problem with this law, for Michener, is that it allows government officials to trespass, to "snoop," on commercial property without probable cause. In doing so, the law gives the bureaucrat too much control over a person's property. By rejecting the Founders' standards of commercial search the law leads to bureaucratic tyranny.

In *Oklahoma Press Publishing Company v. Walling*, the ominous predictions of Congressmen Dondero, Cox and Michener come true. The Oklahoma Press Publishing Company refused to comply with the subpoena from the Labor Department, arguing that as a newspaper it was not covered by the Fair Labor Standards Act, and, furthermore, that any ruling to the contrary violated the First Amendment. Oklahoma Press further argued that being forced to surrender the documents violated the Fourth and Fifth Amendments.[14] The Federal District court issued an order, however, directing the Oklahoma Press Publishing Company to turn over the required documents. The Circuit Court of Appeals affirmed the District Court decision.[15] The Supreme Court granted certiorari,[16] and affirmed the Court of Appeals' decision, rejecting each of the claims of the Oklahoma Press Publishing Company.[17]

For our purposes, what is interesting is the Fourth Amendment aspects of the case. Without providing evidence, the Court argues that, historically, private corporations have been subject to broad visitorial power. The Court states that Congress's right to exercise wide investigative power over corporations (analogous to the visitorial power of the incorporating state), when a corporation's activities occur within, or affect, interstate commerce has long been established.[18] Therefore, the Court concludes, private corporations are not entitled to all of the constitutional protections that private individuals have.[19] The Court admits that the Fourth Amendment has been held applicable to corporations,[20] but argues that under precedent[21] a corporation may be ordered to produce documents.[22] In this instance, the Court says, the search is a "constructive search," which is defined as a request, under subpoena, for documents.[23] As long as the demanding agency is authorized by law to make the inquiry, and as long as the list of items demanded is not overly broad, or unreasonable, the request or subpoena is admissible.[24]

The Court spells out the constitutional requirements of a "constructive search" in the following way:

> It is not necessary, as in the case of a warrant, that a specific charge or complaint of violation of law be pending or that the order be made pursuant to one. It is enough that the investigation be for a lawfully authorized purpose, within the power of Congress to command.... The requirement of 'probable cause supported by oath or affirmation,' literally applicable in the case of a warrant, is satisfied in that of an order for production by the court's determination that the investigation is authorized by Congress, is for a purpose Congress can order, and the documents sought are relevant to the inquiry. Beyond this the requirement of reasonableness, in-

cluding particularity in 'describing the place to be searched, and the persons or things to be seized,' also literally applicable to warrants, comes down to specification of the documents to be produced adequate, but not excessive, for the purposes of the relevant inquiry.[25]

A warrant will not be required: as long as Congress has authorized the inspection of the documents; as long as the inspection is within an area where the Constitution permits Congress to act (i.e., interstate commerce); as long as the inspection agency is authorized to conduct the inspection; and as long as the demand for documents is not too broad—then the "search" is reasonable and may proceed. Notice that neither a warrant nor probable cause is required. Yet, as we have seen, even a warrantless search of an automobile requires probable cause. According to this application of the Fourth Amendment to corporations, businessmen have fewer rights than do suspects in their automobiles.

We see in this decision the beginning of the erosion of protection of corporations against excessive search and seizure. As I discussed earlier, during the New Deal a rapid expansion of Congress' power over the economy and therefore its powers over corporations occurred. The New Deal Congress decided that it should set minimum wage laws in certain industries and occupations, which led it to decide that the federal government has the right to review and inspect the records of industries, by subpoena if necessary. Justice Murphy dissented from the Opinion of the Court in *Oklahoma Press*, alluding to this problem:

> Administrative law has increased greatly in the past few years and seems destined to be augmented even further in the future. But attending this growth should be a new and broader sense of responsibility on the part of administrative agencies and officials.
>
> Excessive use or abuse of authority cannot only destroy man's instinct for liberty but will eventually undo the administrative processes themselves. Our history is not without a precedent of a successful revolt against a ruler who "sent hither swarms of officers to harass our people."[26]

Murphy makes two predictions in this statement. One he gets absolutely right—that administrative law will be greatly augmented in the future.[27] The other has not proven correct, at least so far. The vast expansion of administrative law, an expansion that has led to a diminishing of the Fourth Amendment rights of businessmen has not, as of yet, led to a revolt of the people.

In his dissenting opinion, Justice Murphy argues that it is a mistake to bestow subpoena power upon a non-judicial officer, which is what this procedure does. Even if it is true that the individual who is served with the subpoena may refuse to honor it, it is a fact, Justice Murphy states, that some may yield simply because of the air of authority of the official making the demand. According to Murphy, "Many invasions of private rights thus occur without the restraining hand of the judiciary ever intervening." Therefore, subpoena power must be confined to the judiciary. "Liberty," Justice Murphy concludes, "is too priceless to be forfeited through the zeal of an administrative agent."[28]

Murphy's point is correct as far as it goes. If nothing else, administrative warrants appear to be a massive transfer of power from the judiciary to the executive branch. But Murphy misses the real problem. Even if the subpoenas always required judicial approval before they were released, there would be a problem with the statute. The statute would still allow the administrator, although now with the approval of a federal judge, to search a company's books, records and papers in order to secure evidence against that company without a prior charge or complaint.[29] Completely ignored is the idea that probable cause should exist before the government conducts a search of this type.

The modern understanding that administrative searches do not require warrants is cemented in 1946 with *Davis v. United States*.[30] The case concerned the search of a New York gasoline station owned by Davis. At the time of the events in the case, Davis was suspected of running a black market in gas. In order to test their suspicion, several law enforcement agents drove to his station, observed it for a while, and then two of the agents drove into the station and asked for gas. Both agents were allowed to buy gas without ration coupons by paying twenty cents above the ceiling price. The employee who sold them the gas said that in doing so she was following Davis's instructions. While she was being questioned Davis returned to the station and was arrested. The officers demanded and received the keys to a tin box on top of the gasoline pumps in which were kept the gasoline ration coupons. The agents determined that the gasoline coupons found in the tin boxes were not sufficient to cover the amount of gas emptied from the pumps. When told of this discrepancy, Davis assured the agents that he had a sufficient number of coupons in an inner office of the station to cover the shortage. The agents then demanded entry, based on the fact that the coupons were property of the U.S. government. Davis refused entry, but relented when the agents threatened to break down the door. While the two agents were trying to convince Davis to open the door, another agent shined a flashlight through an outside window of the inner room and appeared to be trying to raise the window. According to one of the agents, when Davis saw this he stated, "He don't need to do that. I will open the damned door."[31] In the room the agents found coupons and used the evidence to convict Davis of unlawful possession of gas rationing coupons. Davis made a motion to exclude the coupons as evidence, claiming the search was a violation of his rights under the Fourth Amendment. The federal district court disagreed and allowed the evidence to be used. Davis was convicted and his appeal was denied by the Court of Appeals. The case was then appealed to the U.S. Supreme Court.[32]

Noted civil libertarian Justice Douglas wrote the Opinion of the Court. Justice Douglas said that the search was not for private papers, but government documents (gas coupons), since the gas coupons at all times remained property of the government and were subject to inspection and recall.[33] Douglas also argues that since the coupons were never Davis's property, but always remained the property of the government, the government had more latitude in conducting its search:

> For an owner who seeks to take it (his property) from one who is unlawfully in possession has long been recognized to have greater leeway than he would have but for his right to possession. The claim of ownership will even justify a trespass and warrant steps otherwise unlawful.[34]

The owner of the property can take extraordinary steps, may even trespass, to retake the property. The government, therefore, was within its rights if it did use extraordinary measures to regain possession of the property. Justice Douglas also seems to suggest that there is a difference between the Fourth Amendment protection that a home and a place of business receives:

> the filling station was a place of business, not a private residence. The right to inspect existed....The public character of property, the fact that the demand was made during business hours at the place of business where the coupons were required to be kept, the existence of the right to inspect, the nature of the request, the fact that the initial refusal to turn the coupons over was soon followed by acquiescence in the demand—these circumstances all support the conclusion of the District Court [to allow the evidence to be admitted as the fruit of a constitutional search].[35]

Part of the reason, therefore, that the Court upheld the search as constitutional is the fact that the search occurred at a place of business. Without explanation, Douglas suggests that the public nature of a business lessens its Fourth Amendment protection. Commentator Scott Bullock has pointed out that here in *Davis* the administrative inspection exception to the Fourth Amendment is born. As Bullock points out, and as I have noted earlier, to search private property government officials must ordinarily first obtain a search warrant based on probable cause.[36] *Davis* (along with *Oklahoma Press Publishing*) begins to carve out an exception to the warrant requirement for searches of businesses. Searches of homes, and later automobiles, will require warrants. Searches of businesses will not.

In his dissent, Justice Frankfurter asserts the Court's opinion seems to make a drastic break with the whole history of the Fourth Amendment:

> [A]...fundamental issue lurks in the Court's opinion if a causal but explicit phrase about the locus of the search and seizure as "a place of business, not a private residence" is intended to carry relevant legal implications. If this is an indirect way of saying that the Fourth Amendment only secures homes against unreasonable searches and seizures but not offices—private offices of physicians and lawyers, of trade unions and other organizations, of business and scientific enterprises—then indeed it would constitute a sudden and drastic break with the whole history of the Fourth Amendment and its applications by this Court....I cannot believe that a vast area of civil liberties was thus meant to be wiped out by a few words without prior argument or consideration.[37]

In an appendix Frankfurter supplies us with a long list of Congressional laws showing that, with a couple of exceptions, Congress required warrants for searches of places, while often specifically exempting searches of vehicles and vessels from the warrant requirement.[38] And, Frankfurter argues that the common law allowed only certain exceptions from the warrant requirement:

> One would expect a hard-headed system like the common law to recognize exceptions even to the most comprehensive principle for safeguarding liberty. This is true of the prohibition of all searches and seizures as unreasonable unless authorized by a judicial warrant appropriately supported. Such is the exception, historically well recognized of the right to seize without warrant goods and pa-

pers on ships or other moving vehicles. Another exception is the right of searching the person upon arrest.[39]

According to Justice Frankfurter, the common law only allows certain exceptions to the warrant requirement, among them vehicle searches. All other searches, including searches on business property, traditionally required warrants.

Justice Frankfurter is also concerned with the Court's acceptance of the government's contention that since the coupons were government property the government may take extraordinary steps in retrieving the property. Frankfurter argues that if the coupons had been properly seized they could have been used in trial. Nevertheless, the fact that the coupons in Davis's possession were government property does not make an otherwise unreasonable search and seizure warranted. Frankfurter argues that the acceptance of this line of argument could lead to immense invasions of privacy.[40] Gasoline coupons, he points out, are not the only documents in the possession of private individuals:

> Only the other day every person not in the armed forces had in his possession O.P.A. documents which technically were the property of the O.P.A. and the same situation may come to pass tomorrow; most businesses in the country are in possession of documents required to be kept under federal and Stat authority; *and there is every prospect that this network of required records will be extended.*[41]

Although he does not elaborate on it, Justice Frankfurter stumbles upon an important point. Under the Court's reasoning, as the federal government expands its power and becomes more involved in people's everyday lives, citizens's protection against the power of the federal government contracts (something we see in the *Oklahoma Press Publishing* case). As Justice Frankfurter notes, the Court in its opinion "apparently rules that because the gasoline business was subject to regulation, the search and seizure ... without a warrant is not an unreasonable search and seizure...."[42] Indeed, possession of government documents, documents that the government in some cases requires you to have, is license for the government to conduct an otherwise unreasonable search and seizure.

Conclusion:
Progressivism, The New Deal and the Fourth Amendment

The change in Fourth Amendment commercial jurisprudence occurs after the New Deal judges assume their places on the Court and this change in Fourth Amendment jurisprudence is part of what can be called the New Deal judicial revolution.[43] The New Deal is itself an outgrowth of early twentieth century Progressivism that called into question the principles of the American Founding, individualism, and property rights.

Among the leading Progressives were Charles Beard, Herbert Croly and John Dewey. Herbert Croly wrote a book, *The Promise of American Life*, which, while mostly forgotten today, was very influential in its time. Croly argues that America must change its notion of private property:

> A democracy dedicated to individual and social betterment is necessarily individualist and socialist....it has the deepest interest in the development of a higher quality of individual self-expression. There are two indispensable economic conditions of qualitative individual self-expression. One is the preservation of the institution of private property in some form, *and the other is the radical transformation of its existing nature and influence.*[44]

Croly and other Progressives believed that "a democracy dedicated to individual and social betterment" is incompatible with the existing social conditions. The current system of property laws allows people, if left to their own devices, to pursue their individual aims unhindered, and so create a great inequality of wealth within society. Croly calls American democracy one of "indiscriminate individualism."[45] In a more humane system the government assures an equable distribution of wealth:

> A democracy certainly cannot fulfill its mission without the eventual assumption by the state of many functions now performed by individuals and without becoming expressly responsible for an improved distribution of wealth.[46]

The Progressive argument holds that we need a government bureaucracy to implement the redistribution of wealth. Democracy requires the administrative state to enforce economic democracy, since political democracy is not an adequate enough means of accomplishing this redistribution.

How does government redistribute income? Through high rates of taxation, primarily. This taxation, the Progressives claim, is not bad for the wealthy, but actually good for them:

> The multimillionaire cannot possibly spend his income save by a recourse to wild and demoralizing extravagance, and in some instances not even extravagance is sufficient for the purpose.[47]

The system of private property and limited government is bad for the rich as well as the poor. Since the rich do not know how to spend their money well, they need the government to step in and protect them from themselves. Croly even says the wealthy have a duty to turn their money over to the state:

> If wealth, particularly when accumulated in large amounts, has a public function, and if its possession imposes a public duty, a society is foolish to leave such a duty to the accidental good intentions of individuals. It should be assumed and should be efficiently performed by the state.[48]

Developing this line of reasoning, Croly suggests that property is not a natural right that the state must protect. Property is created, or allowed to accumulate, by the law of the state; therefore, the state has a right to condition the use of that property.[49]

Another progressive, John Dewey, criticizes the natural-rights liberalism of the founders:

> The real fallacy lies in the notion that individuals have such a native or original endowment of rights, powers and wants that all that is required on the side of institutions and laws is to eliminate the obstructions they offer to the "free" play of the natural equipment of individuals.[50]

The fallacy of the old liberals, that is people like our Founders, was the belief that people had natural rights and to protect those rights limited government was necessary. Times change, Dewey notes, and our political institutions and political ideas must change with them.[51] While limited government may have been all right for our forefathers, things are different now. According to Dewey, we need new ideas to relate to new times, one of these being what he calls "economic revision."[52] And what is this economic revision? It is a socialized economy:

> socialized economy is the means of free individual development as the end.[53]

Unfortunately, Dewey says, Americans treat the ideas of the Founders, for instance the belief in the good of private property, like sacred ideas, forming a religious attachment to these old beliefs. This dedication to the Founders leads to a unwillingness, among the people, to change the institutions of government institutions to keep up with changing economic conditions. Changing economic conditions that allow, for example, for the development of large corporations. The belief in the sacred right of private property prevents necessary reforms, like socializing the economy, that are required by modern conditions.[54] As Thomas West has pointed out, Dewey saw unchecked private control of property as a form of tyranny:

> Dewey wanted government to take control of private property, because "private control of the new forces of production . . . . would operate in the same way as private control of political power..." That is, it would be tyranny. The Founders thought that within the limits just mentioned, life should be permitted to go on spontaneously in families, neighborhoods, and local communities. Dewey thought that a just social order "cannot be established by an unplanned and external convergence of the actions of separate individuals." Only "organized social planning, put into effect for the creation of an order in which industry and finance are socially directed" will allow liberalism to "realize its professed aims."[55]

Far from being a positive good, this belief in private property is a drawback to preventing necessary social change.

The Progressive movement had an immense influence on the New Deal. In his book, *Corporatism and the Rule of Law*, Donald Brand points out that the New Deal shares the tenets of the Progressive movement, including a distrust of laissez-faire economics and its attendant political order, and a belief that a bureaucratic state is necessary to carry out progressive reforms.[56] To implement the New Deal and to achieve economic justice, the Progressives believed the administrative state, a rule by bureaucratic elites, was needed:

> neither group [pragmatists and progressive reformers] regarded the Constitution as it had been understood by its framers as a suitable foundation for governance in the first decades of the twentieth century . . . both groups believed that modern governance required broad discretionary grants of power to governing elites, and each was reluctant to hamstring government with many of the traditional constraints associated with constitutionalism and the rule of

law.[57]

The New Dealers railed against the "economic tyranny" of the rich, and President Franklin Roosevelt proposed the use of "the organized power of government" to combat rich property owners.[58] With the New Deal, Roosevelt "initiated a revolution both in constitutional government and in the American conception of individual rights."[59] For the Progressives, business, in particular big business, is the enemy of justice and the public good and therefore must be controlled by the government. The New Deal philosophy required a government strong enough to fight big business bureaucrats to overcome the selfishness of individualism. The concern changes from one of protecting citizens from an overbearing government, to protecting people from over-powerful, or big, business. And government becomes the protector of the people, instead of a potential source of subjugation. One way government can regulate business is through search of business premises. The rise of progressivism, therefore, leads to a change in thinking about Fourth Amendment searches. Or at least searches of commercial property. The warrant requirement for searches would have to go by the wayside so government could better regulate this economic tyranny. So instead of the old standard of a warrant, warrantless searches of commercial property, as we have seen, develop in the progressive era. Next chapter we shall see the development of the "administrative search warrant" (a warrant that can be issued without probable cause) and the "closely regulated business exception" to the warrant standard (allowing warrantless searches of businesses that are "closely regulated" by government). As I have shown, the purpose of the Fourth Amendment was to protect property owners from unjustified government intrusions. With the rise of progressivism these Fourth Amendment protections are weakened in the name of effective government regulation. The rise of government regulation leads to a de-emphasis of property rights and Fourth Amendment rights of businessmen.

CHAPTER 7

THE RISE OF THE ADMINISTRATIVE STATE AND THE RETURN OF THE GENERAL WARRANT

In the last chapter I discussed the rise in the 1940s of the warrantless administrative search. By the 1960s this development worried some judges. Instead of returning to the original standard of the warrant preference, however, judges devised the administrative warrant for searches of commercial property. Except for searches of so-called closely regulated industries (industries that, as we will see,[1] are closely regulated by the federal government, and therefore, according to the Supreme Court, may be searched without a warrant) searches of commercial property require an administrative warrant. However, with the growth of government regulations, the closely regulated industry exception quickly becomes the rule. The Courts and other governmental actors consider more and more industries "closely regulated," and therefore subject to the "exception" allowing warrantless searches. In addition, the administrative warrant itself is suspect, because it does not require probable cause. In other words, it is a general warrant – the very injustice that the Founders were trying to prevent by adopting the Fourth Amendment.

Some scholars believe the administrative warrant is a good idea. James Haddad, for example, thinks the decision in *Camera v. Munici-*

pal Court [2] (which developed the administrative warrant, and which I will address shortly) correctly weighs and accounts for the interests of society and the individual:

> If the *Camera* dissenters had prevailed, thus allowing search warrants to issue only upon a showing of traditional crime and search probable cause, then the Fourth Amendment's warrant clause in many cases would prevent striking a proper balance between the rights of the citizen and the needs of society.[3]

Haddad is afraid that if judges are not given the option of issuing warrants on less than probable cause in some situations, for example, those involving searches for fingerprints, they will begin to sanction warrantless searches rather than deny the search altogether. In some cases the law enforcement agency cannot realistically establish probable cause for the search. In those cases a warrant based on less than probable cause is preferable to a warrantless search or seizure. At least in the former cases, there is some prior judicial approval and knowledge.

Haddad is correct that in some cases it would not be reasonable to require a warrant for a search, for example, in using airline metal detectors. The Fourth Amendment, however, already provides for this through the reasonableness clause. There is no need to gut the warrant clause for these situations. And Haddad does not state why it would be unreasonable, except in exigent circumstances, for the government to be required to get a warrant based on probable cause to search a building, as the Founding generation intended.

The judiciary, and scholars such as Haddad, surrenders the Fourth Amendment rights of businessmen to the needs of the administrative state. As I will show, it is no mistake that the general warrant returns with the growth of the administrative state. As government becomes stronger and more intrusive, as it gains more and more control over property,[4] it must come up with greater and more intrusive means of regulating that property.

The cases that lead to the development of the administrative warrant are the companion cases of *See v. City of Seattle*,[5] and *Camera v. Municipal Court of the City and County of San Francisco*. *See* involved the administrative inspection of commercial buildings, while *Camera* was concerned with warrantless inspections of dwellings for housing code violations. Although *Camera* is the more famous of the two cases, because *See* concerns the issue of commercial searches, I will examine it first.

THE RISE OF THE ADMINISTRATIVE STATE AND THE   79
RETURN OF THE GENERAL WARRANT

See was convicted for refusing to let a representative of the City of Seattle Fire Department enter and inspect his warehouse without a warrant, and without probable cause to believe any violation of any city ordinance existed in the warehouse. The inspection was conducted as part of a routine citywide examination of property to insure compliance with the city fire code. After he refused entry to the inspector, See was arrested for violating a city ordinance that required that the city fire inspector be admitted to all buildings, "except the interiors of dwellings," to check for fire code violations. See was convicted and the Supreme Court of the State of Washington affirmed the conviction, arguing that in *Davis v. United States* the U.S. Supreme Court had applied different standards of reasonableness to searches of dwellings and to businesses. The U.S. Supreme Court agreed to hear See's appeal and reversed the conviction.[6]

The Court argued that a businessman, like the occupant of a dwelling, has the right to be free from unreasonable official entries upon his property. Furthermore, the Court argued that this right is placed in jeopardy when a government official can inspect the businessman's property without a warrant.[7] Citing *Oklahoma Press Publishing*, the Court argued that if a so-called constructive search requires a subpoena that is "limited in scope, relevant in purpose, and specific in directive" so that it is not unreasonably burdensome,[8] and if the subpoenaed party may seek judicial review of reasonableness before the subpoena is issued, then an actual search must also be subject to similar requirements. In other words, if the businessman objects to the search, the government officials must go to court to obtain a warrant before they can conduct the search.[9]

The decision is not as great a victory for commercial property owners as one may think. The most pernicious aspect of this decision is its rejection of the Fourth Amendment requirement for probable cause for administrative warrants. The Court states that the "agency's particular demand for access will of course be measured, in terms of probable cause to issue a warrant, against a flexible standard of reasonableness that takes into account the public need for effective enforcement of the particular regulation involved."[10] The standard for an administrative warrant is not probable cause that a violation has taken place, but the "need for effective enforcement of a particular regulation." What this means may be best brought to light by looking at the case of *Camera v. Municipal Court of the City and County of San Francisco*.

In *Camera*, the Supreme Court ruled that a warrant was required to conduct a housing inspection if the occupant refused entry to an inspector. However, the warrant, the Court said, did not have to be based on probable cause:

> In determining whether a particular inspection is reasonable—and thus in determining whether there is probable cause to issue a warrant for that inspection—the need for the inspection must be weighed in terms of these reasonable goals of code enforcement.[11]

A warrant will be issued if the inspection is deemed reasonable. The fact that the inspection is reasonable satisfies the probable cause requirement of the warrant clause of the Fourth Amendment. In contrast to the search of a home, in this case the government does not have to establish probable cause—it only has to establish that the inspection is reasonable.

The Court gives three reasons why searches by administrative agencies are different from other searches. First, the Court claims, administrative searches have long been accepted by the judiciary and the public. Second, public interest demands that dangerous conditions be prevented and an administrative search is the best method to prevent, detect and remedy these dangerous conditions. Finally, the Court argues, administrative searches pass constitutional muster because the inspections are neither personal in nature nor aimed at the discovery of evidence of crime, and because they involve a relatively limited invasion of the citizen's privacy.[12] In making this distinction between regular searches and those conducted by administrative agencies, the Court allows the criminal, or more correctly the suspected criminal, more rights than the average citizen or businessman. Since the search of the suspected criminal's place or dwelling is usually going to involve the attempted discovery of the evidence of a crime, a warrant with probable cause is necessary. However, since the administrative search, or inspection, is not concerned with the discovery of criminal evidence, that is, because the subject of the search is a law-abiding citizen, a warrant may be necessary, but probable cause is not.

Just what the Court means in modifying the probable cause standard can be seen in its approving quotation of Justice Douglas's dissent in *Frank v. Maryland*.[13] The quotation from Douglas ends with these sentences:

> The passage of a certain period without inspection might of itself be sufficient in a given situation to justify the issuance of a warrant. The test of 'probable cause' required by the Fourth Amendment can take into account the nature of the search.[14]

For administrative searches the probable cause requirement of the warrant clause is not just relaxed, it is abolished. A search is reasonable—and therefore under the administrative search standard constitutes probable cause—if a certain period has passed. The justification for this standard is the public interest:

> The warrant procedure is designed to guarantee that a decision to search private property is justified by a reasonable governmental interest. But, reasonableness is still the ultimate standard. If a valid public interest justifies the intrusion contemplated, then there is probable cause to issue a suitably restricted search warrant.[15]

Public interest itself becomes the probable cause. And who determines whether the search is in the public's interest? The executive, and (if the administrative agency's decision is appealed) the judicial branches of the very government that is searching. As Susan McDonough has put it:

> the court [in *Camera*] defers to administrative standards and procedures to define reasonableness. The purpose of administrative agencies is to protect the public interest; consequently, the functions and procedures of an agency are consistently viewed as per se reasonable, never tipping the scale to afford Fourth Amendment protections.[16]

We see in the decisions of *See* and *Camera* a further weakening of constitutional protections. While there are many different interpretations of the Fourth Amendment, with some scholars emphasizing the warrant clause and others the reasonableness clause, almost all agree that if a warrant is going to be used, probable cause must be demonstrated before the warrant is to be issued. As the amendment clearly states, "no warrants shall issue, but upon probable cause."[17] Silas Wasserstrom and Louis Seidman state the case thusly:

> The amendment by its terms requires neither probable cause nor warrants for searches and seizures, but it does require probable cause for all warrants. Yet the Court has insisted on both probable cause and warrants for many searches, while declining to enforce the clear textual prohibition against warrants issued on less than probable cause.[18]

The Fourth Amendment is turned upside down in the twentieth century. Searches that traditionally did not require warrants (of criminal suspects in public areas) suddenly must have one. On the other hand, when it comes to searches of commercial property, in some cases, clear textual requirements are being ignored. It is as if the courts are bending over backwards to strengthen the protections of criminal suspects and to lessen the protections of businessmen.

The More the Regulation, the Less the Protection? *Colonnade* and *Biswell*

The two cases *Colonnade* and *Biswell* are important because they involve the claim that industries that traditionally have been highly regulated by government may not have the Fourth Amendment protections afforded to other businesses. As we shall see, the argument is that if one enters into an industry that traditionally involves a high degree of government regulation, one implicitly consents to stricter governmental controls, including warrantless searches.[19]

Colonnade Catering Corporation v. United States[20] involves inspections of liquor stores. Federal agents visited Colonnade's business while a party was taking place,[21] noticed the serving of liquor, and, without the manager's consent, inspected the cellar. The agents demanded the opening of the liquor storeroom. The president of the corporation arrived and refused to comply, and asked to see a search warrant. When the agents stated that they did not have one, the president again refused to open the storeroom, whereupon the agents broke the lock and entered. They removed bottles of liquor that they suspected were refilled contrary to U.S. Code.

Under The Internal Revenue Code of 1958, the Secretary of Treasury or his delegate has the authority to enter the premises and inspect the records of retail dealers in liquors.[22] If the person owning or having superintendence over the building refuses entry, another section of the Code provides for a fine of $500.[23] The question for the Court was whether the fine was to be the exclusive sanction for refusal to allow entry.[24] The Court said that it was. The Court argued that Congress has the authority to design the powers of inspection and the remedies of violations of inspection laws.[25] According to the Court, because of the long history in this country of allowing warrantless searches on premises that sold liquor to enforce liquor excise taxes,[26] the rule of *See v. City of Seattle* "that administrative entry, without consent, upon the portions of commercial premises which are not open to the public may only be compelled through prosecution or physical force within the framework of a warrant procedure" is not applicable in this case.²⁷ Congress, if it wanted, could have permitted warrantless searches of liquor stores. However, the Court argued, Congress chose another approach, i. e., fining establishments that refused to allow searches. Therefore, warrantless searches of liquor establishments are not permitted. If officers are refused permission to search the establishment they have another remedy—the fine.

What at first appears here to be a victory for businesses in the area of search and seizure, on reflection does not seem so at all. The Court denies the validity of the warrantless search, not because warrantless searches of business is against the Fourth Amendment, but because there is another Congressionally sanctioned remedy available to federal law enforcement officers. The warrantless search would be acceptable, at least in the case of liquor establishments, had Congress sanctioned it, because the federal government traditionally has already regulated liquor establishments. The more government is involved in one's business; it seems, the less, not more, protection one receives. Furthermore, the Court acquiesces in Congress's punishing people for exercising their constitutional rights. The law calls for a fine of five hundred dollars if the storeowner or manager refuses entry to liquor inspectors. The Fourth Amendment protects citizens from unwarranted, government intrusions on our property, yet the law punishes the liquor storeowners for refusing to allow a warrantless search.[28] I suppose one could argue that liquor is a special case, since liquor has often been seen a corrupting influence in need of special government regulation (prohibition, drinking age, blue laws, etc.). Yet this does not justify violation of the Fourth Amendment. Government officials should be able to search liquor businesses, but only when there was probable cause that a violation had occurred.

In the 1972 case of *United States v. Biswell*,[29] the Supreme Court expands this closely regulated industry exception by stating that an industry does not require a long history of government regulation to be subject to warrantless searches. The Court held that a warrantless search of a locked storeroom during business hours did not violate the Fourth Amendment. The Gun Control Act of 1968 (82 Stat. 1213) authorized official entry during business hours into the premises of firearms dealers for the purpose of inspecting any firearms ammunition, and records or documents kept at the location.[30] Biswell owned a pawnshop and had a federal license to deal in sporting weapons. During an inspection, a federal agent asked, Biswell to open a locked storeroom. When Biswell asked whether the agent had a warrant, the agent replied that under the Gun Control Act he did not need one. Biswell unlocked the storeroom and the agent found two sawed-off shotguns for which Biswell did not have licenses. He was indicted and convicted of dealing in firearms without having paid a special occupational tax. On appeal, the U. S. Court of Appeals ruled that Section 923(g) was unconstitutional because it subjected businesses to warrantless searches. The Supreme Court granted certiorari.[31]

The Supreme Court reversed the court of appeals' decision. The Court argued that when the officers asked to inspect the storeroom they were merely asserting their statutory right, and, remarkably, found this situation analogous to a householder's acquiescence in a search pursuant to a *warrant*. In neither case does the lawfulness of the search depend on consent. The officer has the right to search the house, not because of the consent of the owner, but because of the warrant. Likewise, the agent has the right to search the storeroom, not because the pawnshop owner consented, but because of the statutory authority. The Court stated that "(I)n the context of a regulatory inspection system of business premises that is carefully limited in time, place, and scope, the legality of the search depends not on consent but on the authority of a valid statue."[32] A warrant is required to search the home, while in the case of a business all that is required is statutory authority. If Congress decides that an industry should be closely regulated, and as part of that regulation warrantless searches are required, under *Biswell* these warrantless searches are permissible. To search a home the government must go before a judge, demonstrate probable cause, and obtain a warrant. Under *Biswell*, if Congress deems an industry "closely regulated" and authorizes by statute warrantless searches it is constitutional. Businesses will have less protection than other places.

Colonnade and *Biswell* form the "closely regulated industry exception" to the warrant requirement.[33] The exception "holds that one consents to reasonable forms of governmental intrusion to further a legitimate and necessary governmental interest when one engages in certain highly regulated industries."[34] As could almost be expected, the closely regulated business exception has increased over time to cover almost any business:

> legislators and regulators decided what would be closely regulated and how to gain the power to search. And, in the cases that followed [*Colonnade and Biswell*], the Court granted great deference to legislative determination that a particular industry is to be "closely regulated," whether truly necessary or not. Thus, this exception began to greatly expand.[35]

THE RISE OF THE ADMINISTRATIVE STATE AND THE RETURN OF THE GENERAL WARRANT

As John Wesley Hall puts it later in his study, "[t]he cases first indicated that a persuasive and historical scheme was required [*Colonnade*] but, in much later cases, it was sufficient for the government simply to articulate its perceived need for intrusion to make it so."[36] When a person enters a business in which there is a "weighty public interest," he or she implicitly consents to warrantless inspections.[37] Moreover, weighty public interest, as Hall points out, has been expanded to cover any business that the government chooses to include. As the *Burger* case shows, the administrative warrant probable cause exception can cover almost any business. Attorney Steven Wax sums up the situation nicely:

> The specific holding [in *Biswell*] was limited to situations in which the regulatory inspections would "further urgent federal interest[s], and the possibilities of abuse and the threat to privacy are not of impressive dimensions." Put in somewhat less legal terms, the essence of the holding is that when the federal government's interest is strong enough, the citizen is required to trust that there will be no abuse in the absence of judicial intervention.[38]

In the *Biswell* case the Court acknowledges that firearm inspections are not deeply rooted in the regulatory history, but states that such inspections are permissible because of the greater public good that is served (the prevention of violent crime).[39] Therefore, when a dealer chooses to enter the firearms business he should realize the business is closely regulated and accept the regulatory scheme as the price of doing business. To do business the government requires a license, and a condition of receiving that license is accepting effective government regulation. As Eileen Dribin says:

> The evils of the search allowed here go beyond those envisioned by the framers of the Fourth amendment. Even the writs of assistance did not go this far, but only authorized examination of premises to seize goods on which duty had not been paid. Here the government can search not only to seize, but also to obtain evidence to use in criminal proceedings.[40]

Under this Supreme Court decision effective government regulation means warrantless inspections. For the government—sanctioned right to do business, one must surrender part of one's constitutional rights. Again we see that the more regulated the business the less protected it is. To quote Eileen Dribin again, "the practical effect of *Biswell* is clear: a dealer who with notice enters a closely controlled industry regulated by a precise statute defining time, place and scope of search may expect regular, unannounced invasions of his business privacy."[41]

The Tide Begins to Turn?: *G.M. Leasing* and *Barlow's*

In the late 1970s the Court hands down decisions in two important commercial search cases, *G.M. Leasing Corporation, v. United States*[42] and *Marshall, Secretary of Labor, et al. v. Barlow's, Inc.*[43] Both of these cases strike down warrantless searches of businesses. At first glance, then, they seem to be victories for business. Upon closer inspection, however, we see that both cases are in fact hollow victories. In *G. M. Leasing* the Court acknowledges that businessmen do not have the Fourth Amendment protections of other individuals, and in *Barlow's* the Court strengthens the probable cause exception of the administrative warrant. Both decisions are setbacks for the Fourth Amendment protection of commercial property.

In *G.M. Leasing* the Internal Revenue Service seized the assets of the G. M. Leasing corporation, which was controlled by George Norman, a federal tax delinquent and a fugitive from justice. Revenue officers, without a warrant, seized vehicles owned by the corporation. The agents, again without a warrant, and with the aid of a locksmith, then entered the corporation office and removed furnishings and documents. The corporation filed suit for the return of the documents, and the Internal Revenue Service did return them—after first photocopying them. The G. M. Leasing Corporation sued for damages.

The Supreme Court declared that probable cause existed for the search and seizures. The only issues, it said, were whether warrants were necessary to make reasonable the seizure of the vehicles, the entry into the office, and the seizure of goods therein.[44]

As for the warrantless seizure of the vehicles, the Court kept to the original understanding. The Court argued that the actions of the federal officers were legal, since the vehicle seizures occurred on public streets, in parking lots and in other open places that did not involve any invasion of privacy. Citing an 1856 case, *Murray's Lessee v. Hoboken Land & Improv. Co.*,[45] the Court stated that a judicial warrant was not needed to seize possessions, if the seizure does not involve the invasion of privacy.

When the Court comes to the search in the office, however, it presents a different story. The Court notes that the government does not deny that businessmen have Fourth Amendment protection.[46] However the Court states that the Fourth Amendment rights of businessmen differ from the Fourth Amendment rights of others:

> The Court, of course, has recognized that a business, by its special nature and voluntary existence, may open itself to intrusions that would not be permissible in a purely private context.[47]

The nature of one's business, such as the sale of firearms or liquor, opens one up to more government inspection and leads to a weakening of one's constitutional protections. The Court found, however, that the search and seizure did not occur because of the nature of the business, but for the seizure of assets to satisfy tax assessments. In other words, what is involved is the normal enforcement of tax laws, and here the Court finds no reason for treating a corporation any differently than an individual.[48]

The most interesting aspect of this case is that the government argued that there is a broad exception to the Fourth Amendment that permits warrantless searches and seizures in tax cases. The Court says that it recognizes that Article I, Section 8 of the Constitution gives the federal government the power to lay and collect taxes, and that the First Congress—which proposed the Bill of Rights—also enacted a law providing that taxes could be levied by distress and sale of goods of the person or persons refusing to pay. The act, the Court argued, related to warrantless seizures, not warrantless searches, and:

> It is one thing to seize without a warrant property resting in an open area or seizable by levy without an intrusion into privacy, and it is quite another thing to effect a warrantless seizure of property, even that owned by a corporation, situated on private premises to which access is not otherwise available for the seizing officer.[49]

Far from there being a tax enforcement exception to the Fourth Amendment, the Court points out that one of the primary purposes of the Fourth Amendment was to keep tax collectors from overstepping their bounds. The Opinion of the Court quotes, in part, James Madison's speech to the House of Representatives in which he urges the passage of the Bill of Rights:

> The General Government has a right to pass all laws which shall be necessary to collect its revenue; the means for enforcing the collection are within the direction of the Legislature: may not gen-

eral warrants be considered necessary for this purpose, as well as for some purposes which it was supposed at the framing of their constitutions the State Governments had in view? If there was reason for restraining the State Governments from exercising this power, there is like reason for restraining the Federal Government.[50]

The Court states that there is no clear evidence in the historical record to suggest that tax enforcement should constitute an exception from Fourth Amendment protections against warrantless searches.[51]

The final point the Court makes is in response to the government's claim that the warrantless search is legal because it is authorized by congressional statute. The statute, The Internal Revenue Code of 1954,[52] authorizes seizure by any means. The government argued that this included warrantless searches. The Court rejected that argument, and suggested that the government offered no legislative history to support its position. If the Court were to adopt the government's position, tax enforcement officers could invade both businesses and dwellings to conduct warrantless searches. The Court decides to give the statute what it calls its "natural reading"—that the statute allows for all forms of seizures and is silent on the question of intrusions into privacy. Since the statute is silent, the normal Fourth Amendment standard is the rule. And that standard is that "'except in certain carefully defined classes of cases, a search of private property without proper consent is 'unreasonable' unless it has been authorized by a valid search warrant.'"[53]

In this case the Court accepts the current notion that the privacy rights of businesses are not as strong as individuals, and the Court is willing to concede that businesses do not have the Fourth Amendment protections that individuals in their homes have. This aspect of modern jurisprudence does not change. The Court simply states (as earlier Courts had) that businesses have *some* Fourth Amendment rights. Among those protections for business people is the right against warrantless searches of business premises for tax enforcement.

In *Marshall, Secretary of Labor, et al. v. Barlow's, Inc.* the Court invalidates a warrantless search of a business. Nevertheless, as we will see, it strengthens the probable cause exception for administrative search warrants. Here is another instance of a seeming victory that is actually a defeat. Barlow's Inc. was an electrical and plumbing installation business that challenged Section 8(a) of the Occupational Safety and Health Act of 1970.[54] The act gave agents of the Federal Depart-

THE RISE OF THE ADMINISTRATIVE STATE AND THE 89
RETURN OF THE GENERAL WARRANT

ment of Labor the power to search the work area of any business in OSHA's area of jurisdiction for violations of worker safety regulations. No search warrant was required under the act.[55]

An inspector from OSHA arrived at Barlow's to conduct such an investigation. Barlow, the president of the company asked the agent if any complaint concerning worker safety had been received about the company. The inspector said no, Barlow's had simply turned up in the agency's selection process. Barlow then asked if the agent had a search warrant. The agent said no and Barlow refused entry, citing the Fourth Amendment.[56]

The Secretary of Labor then petitioned the federal district court for an order compelling the company to admit the inspector. The court granted the order, but Barlow refused entry and sought injunctive relief against the warrantless searches by OSHA. A three—judge federal panel ruled in favor of Barlow, and the Secretary of Labor appealed to the U. S. Supreme Court, which agreed to hear the case.[57]

The Secretary of Labor claimed that the Fourth Amendment sanctioned warrantless inspections to enforce OSHA. The Secretary also claimed that Section 8 (a), which allows warrantless inspections of businesses, represented the congressional interpretation of the Fourth Amendment that the Court must respect.[58]

The Supreme Court argued that the Fourth Amendment protected businesses as well as homes. It said to hold otherwise would be to distort the origin of the Fourth Amendment. As the Court pointed out, and as I have noted earlier,[59] the general warrant was one of the colonist's chief complaints against British rule. Among the things the colonists were concerned with were the warrantless searches of businesses:

> The particular offensiveness it engendered was acutely felt by the merchants and businessmen whose premises and products were inspected for compliance with the several parliamentary revenue measures that most irritated the colonists.[60]

According to the Court, this historical background suggests that the Fourth Amendment was meant to protect businesses against warrantless searches.

The Court disagreed with the Secretary of Labor when he urged that the warrantless search is legal under the closely regulated business exception. The Court acknowledged the closely regulated business exception, but held that the exception is for businesses, like liquor and firearms, that have a long history of close government supervision. The person entering such a business must realize he is subject to close governmental scrutiny and consents to it, at least tacitly.[61] The Secretary argued that all businesses involved in interstate commerce have been subject to government supervision when it came to employee safety and health conditions, so in those cases businesses should be subject to warrantless searches. In other words, since most business can be tied to interstate commerce in one way or another, just about all businesses should be subject to warrantless searches. As the Court pointed out, the Secretary takes what had been the exception and attempts to turn it into the rule.[62]

The Secretary of Labor argued that the enforcement of the act required warrantless searches and that since the act had safeguards to protect the privacy of businessmen, searches in the enforcement of the act fell under the reasonableness standard of the Fourth Amendment, and were therefore constitutional.[63] Surprise inspections were needed for the proper enforcement of OSHA regulations. Many unsafe conditions could be altered or disguised if the businessman knew his place of business was about to be inspected.[64]

The Court did not accept this argument. First, the Court argued, most business people will comply with the request for a search. Secondly, Department of Labor regulations at the time of the case required an inspector who was refused entry to a business to report to his superior, thereby giving the businessperson time to alter the condition or conditions at the business.[65] If the Labor Department really believes in the necessity of surprise inspections, why have this regulation? Why not have the inspector stay at the business until a warrant can be issued by a judge (which happens in criminal cases)?

Finally, the Court, using *Camera* as its basis, argued this is not an undue burden on the agency because the agency does not have to demonstrate probable cause to get the warrant:

> Whether the Secretary proceeds to secure a warrant or other process, with or without prior notice, *his entitlement to inspect will not depend on his demonstrating probable cause to believe that conditions in violation of OSHA exist on the premises.* Probable cause in the criminal law sense is not required....A warrant showing that a specific business has been chosen for an OSHA search on the basis of a general administrative plan for the enforcement of the Act derived from neutral sources...would protect the employer's Fourth Amendment rights.[66]

Since no probable cause or particularized suspicion is required, the

Court thus approves an agency's use of the previously condemned general warrant. In Chapter 1 we discussed general warrants. These general warrants inflamed the passions of the colonists because they allowed British officers to search property without a warrant that specifically demonstrated probable cause to search that particular property. Armed with a general warrant, they could search any property where they suspected to find illegal goods. It is this device that so concerned our forefathers and inspired the protections of the Fourth Amendment. With the probable cause exception to the warrant clause of the Fourth Amendment, the general warrant returns when it comes to searches of commercial property. Probable cause is no longer needed to search commercial property.

Barlow's not only reaffirms as constitutional warrantless searches of so-called closely regulated businesses, it also reaffirms the probable cause exception for administrative warrants. With one hand the government gives businesses the protection of the warrant requirement, but then with the other takes away probable cause requirement. All the government will need to get a warrant will be to show that its desire to search a particular business is derived from "neutral sources," i.e., the company was chosen at random to be investigated. In other words, the government cannot target a particular company, or discriminate against an out—of-favor company or industry. But to get a warrant it does not need probable cause either. The government still has the right to search any business it wants. If challenged, all the government has to do is demonstrate that it is treating the business fairly. The diluted search warrant is not much of a search warrant at all, and is not much protection at all.

The Closely Regulated Industry Exception: Does the Exception Swallow the Rule?

Earlier in this chapter, I noted an exception to the warrant requirement for industries, which justified a warrantless search when there had been a long history of government regulation, or manifest need. In *Donovan, Secretary of Labor v. Dewey* [67] and *New York v. Burger*[68] the Court greatly expands the closely regulated industry exception to cover almost any industry.

The Donovan in *Donovan v. Dewey* is Ray Donovan, notorious in some circles as the conservative Labor Secretary during the first Reagan administration. The secretary filed suit demanding that his department be allowed to conduct a warrantless search of a business. This is instructive—even conservatives – who have the reputation of being pro-business, have seemingly abandoned the concern for the Fourth Amendment rights of businessmen.

Section 103(a) of the Federal Mine Safety and Health Act authorized warrantless inspections of under-ground and surface mines. Federal mine inspectors, according to the act, are to inspect underground mines four times a year and surface mines twice a year, not including follow—up inspections if any violations are found. The act states that no advance notice need be given. If the mine owner refuses to allow the warrantless inspection, the Secretary of Labor can go to court to seek an order demanding that the mine owner allow the inspection.[69]

In June of 1978, a federal mine inspector returned to the quarries owned by Waukesha Lime and Stone Company to determine whether the company had corrected health and safety problems found in an earlier inspection. After the inspector had been on the property about an hour, the president of Waukesha, Dewey, refused to allow him to continue without a warrant. The inspector and the Department of Labor went to court to seek relief. Federal district court ruled in favor of Dewey because warrantless searches of property violated the Fourth Amendment. The Secretary of Labor appealed directly to the U. S. Supreme Court, and the Court agreed to take the case.[70]

The Supreme Court ruled that the inspection scheme in the Federal Mine Safety and Health Act was constitutional. The Court stated the government had substantial interest in regulating and improving safety conditions in mines. Congress knew that the mining industry was among the most hazardous in the country and had a serious impact on interstate commerce, and, in preparing the legislation realized that not allowing warrantless inspection would make enforcing the act difficult. The Court quotes the Senate report on the act, which states that, because of the ease of concealing safety violations, "a warrant requirement would seriously undercut this Act's objectives." Quoting *Biswell*, the Court argued that Congress could properly conclude that a warrant requirement would foil inspections, and that the inspection program provides a constitutionally adequate substitute for a warrant.[71] This is true even in the case of stone quarries, which do not have a long history of government regulation, the Court argued.[72]

One could also argue that because of the ease of concealing illegal drugs, a warrant requirement for the search of a vehicle, luggage or person would seriously undercut law enforcement. However, as we have seen, the modern judiciary has not hesitated to exclude drugs taken in warrantless searches of vehicles, luggage or persons, even

THE RISE OF THE ADMINISTRATIVE STATE AND THE 93
RETURN OF THE GENERAL WARRANT

though the original understanding of the Fourth Amendment would have condoned such searches in public areas. As was mentioned earlier, this shows the bias of the modern judiciary in favor of some types of illegal activity (street crime) and against property and the rights of businessmen.

One problem with the ruling in *Donovan*, and the other cases I have examined, is that the more a business is regulated the less protection it has. In his dissenting opinion, Justice Stewart addresses this issue:

> Under the peculiar logic of today's opinion the scope of the Fourth Amendment diminishes as the power of governmental regulations increases. Yet I would have supposed that the mandates of the Fourth Amendment demand heightened, not lowered, respect, as the intrusive regulatory authority of government expands.[73]

The Court held that "Congress had great latitude to determine that a particular type of commercial property required unannounced warrantless inspections."[74] As Justice Stewart also points out, this opens up just about any business for warrantless searches:

> As I read today's opinion, Congress is left free to avoid the Fourth Amendment industry by industry even though the Court held in *Barlow's* that Congress could not avoid that Amendment all at once. Congress after today can define any industry as dangerous, regulate it substantially, and provide for warrantless inspections of its members. But, because I do not believe that Congress can, by legislative fiat, rob the members of any industry of their constitutional protection, I dissent from the opinion and judgment of the Court.[75]

The Court with one fell swoop eliminates the doctrine that warrantless searches of businesses are limited to those that have a long history of extensive governmental regulation. The very people who need the amendment most will lose its protection. All Congress has to do is declare an industry dangerous, regulate it, and you lose some of your Fourth Amendment protections. Businessmen will be treated as second—class citizens. As Steven Wax has said, after *Dewey* "the new formulation required neither a long history of regulation nor an urgent need for federal regulation and inspection. Necessity for regulation would now suffice."[76]

Was Justice Stewart correct in his prediction that more and more industries would become subject to warrantless searches? To answer this I will examine another Supreme Court decision. In *New York v. Burger* the Supreme Court upheld a New York law that provided for warrantless searches of junkyards. Joseph Burger owned a junkyard in Brooklyn, where as part of his business, he dismantled automobiles and sold the parts. In 1982 New York City officers entered the junkyard and asked to see Burger's license and "police book."[77] Burger told the officers he had neither. The officers then told Burger that they were going to conduct an inspection under New York statute 415-a5, which requires junkyard owners to have a license and keep a police book. The statute also allows officers to conduct a warrantless inspection of junkyards in search of stolen vehicles.[78] Burger did not object. The officers found stolen vehicles and charged Burger with possession of stolen property. At his trial, Burger moved to have the evidence suppressed as the fruit of an unreasonable search and seizure, but his motion was denied. The Appellate Division affirmed, but the New York Court of Appeals reversed, saying the search violated the Fourth Amendment. According to the New York Court of Appeals, the law permitted the searches of junkyards. The Supreme Court then granted certiorari.

In this case, the Supreme Court reiterated its position that a businessman in a closely regulated industry has less of an expectation of privacy than do other citizens, and that therefore warrantless searches, if they meet certain criteria, are legitimate.[79] The criteria? First, there must be a substantial government interest. Second, warrantless inspections must be necessary to further the regulatory scheme. Third, the inspection program, through certainty and regularity, must provide an adequate substitution for a warrant. As the Court wrote, "(I)n other words, the regulatory statute must perform the two basic functions of a warrant: it must advise the owner of the commercial premises that the search is being made pursuant to the law and has a properly defined scope, and it must limit the discretion of the inspecting officers."[80] John Wesley Hall notes that, with this ruling, the administrative search exception to probable cause becomes the rule rather than the exception. What is supposed to be the "exception" becomes common practice:

> The "administrative search exception," if it was one, is now, to use Justice Brennan's word, the "rule." By imposing regulation, the government can now impose the warrant exception on practically any industry which it could conceivably regulate. The Court likely did not intend this result, but the breadth of its language and the efforts it goes to support its rationale indicate that this warrant ex-

ception will go practically anywhere the legislatures and city councils want. *Burger* is a legislative blueprint for searches of commercial premises that will be difficult to keep confined to its own limited facts.[81]

The Supreme Court determined that the state of New York correctly designated the junkyard as a closely regulated business. There had not been a long history of government regulation of junkyards simply because the automobile was a relatively late invention.[82] Furthermore, the Supreme Court ruled that the New York statute met all three of the criteria for reasonableness. First, the state has a substantial interest in regulating junkyards because of vehicle theft; second, regulating junkyards reasonably serves state interest in eliminating vehicle theft; and third, the statute provides a constitutionally adequate substitute for a warrant, since it informs the junkyard owner that inspections will be made on a regular basis.[83] The statute also sets forth the scope of the inspection, so the operator may comply fully. It notifies the operator as to who is authorized to conduct the inspection, and the limits on time, place and scope of the inspections.[84] Therefore, the warrantless inspection is constitutional.

Justices Marshall, Brennan and O'Connor filed a dissenting opinion. They admit that warrantless searches of closely regulated businesses are valid. The problem in this case, they argue, is that Burger's vehicle-dismantling business is not closely regulated, unless one could call all businesses closely regulated. The dissenters believe that the Court's opinion renders the administrative search warrant meaningless.[85]

The dissent maintains that the procedures a vehicle dismantler follows to open and stay in business are not extensive. The dismantler has to pay a fee and register, display the registration, maintain a police book and allow inspections. The inspections themselves cannot be a reason for being considered extensively regulated, for that creates a catch-22 situation. As for the other procedures, many businesses in New York face similar regulatory requirements. If vehicle dismantling is considered closely regulated, then almost any business in "closely regulated." The warrantless inspection exception then becomes the rule, not the exception.[86]

The dissenters are particularly concerned because they believe that the New York law allows the state to use the looser standards of administrative searches to conduct criminal searches. The dissent points out that the Court has ruled in numerous cases that the government may not use the administrative search scheme to search for criminal violations, yet that is exactly what the New York law does - it allows administrative searches for stolen property. In fact, in Burger's case, it is obvious that the search was for criminal evidence. At the start of the police visit Burger admits that he did not have a registration or a police book. Before the search had even begun, he had admitted to violating every administrative requirement. There was no need to search, except to uncover stolen property. If the state wanted to search for stolen property, it should have gotten a warrant, using the failure to register and keep a police book as an argument for probable cause—at the same time keeping officers in or around the property to make sure no stolen property disappeared.[87] The dissent sums up its point by stating that:

> on the Court's reasoning, administrative inspections would evade the requirements of the Fourth Amendment so long as they served an abstract administrative goal, such as prevention of automobile theft.[88]

The dissent is right as far as it goes, but seems to miss the big picture. The solution is not to distinguish between administrative and criminal searches of business property, allowing a looser standard (the administrative warrant) for the former and a stricter standard (the regular warrant) for the latter. The better solution, it would seem, would be to require a regular warrant for searching businesses just as one is required for searching dwellings. The dissent does seem, however, to arrive at a correct conclusion:

> The implications of the Court's opinion, if realized, will virtually eliminate Fourth Amendment protection of commercial entities in the context of administrative searches. No State may require, as a condition of doing business, a blanket submission to warrantless searches for any purpose.[89]

True, but the administrative warrant, as we have seen is, in reality, not much better than the warrantless search.

Conclusion:
"Federal Control Is a Two-Edged Sword"

The quotation above may sound familiar. As noted in the previous chapter, Representative Cox made this statement during the debate on the Fair Labor Standards Act. Twentieth-century Fourth Amendment jurisprudence has greatly expanded the government's right to search commercial property. Not coincidentally, federal power has so greatly expanded in the twentieth century. Both this and the previous chapter have shown the price commercial property owners have paid for the expansion of the administrative state. The government, to accomplish its goals, has become more and more intrusive. It has become intrusive to the point that it may conduct a warrantless search of commercial property (the so—called administrative search) simply because it deems it necessary to do so. In pursuit of their definition of justice—which, as I discussed in the last chapter, requires economic socialism—progressives have diminished property protections. If the social good demands the invasion of commercial property, this is for the best. The Founders would have condemned this change, because they would have seen it as unjust. The Virginia Declaration of Rights states that among the rights of mankind is the right "of acquiring and possessing property." John Dickinson, in his *Letters from a Farmer* criticizes the British policy of taxing the colonists without their consent:

> If [the British] have any right to tax us—then, whether our own money shall continue in our own pockets or not, depends no longer on us, but on them. There is nothing which we can call our own; or, to use the words of Mr. Locke—"What property have we in that which another may, by right, take when he pleases to himself?"[90]

Property is something we can call our own. It is something we earn through the sweat of our brows. Since what man acquires and possesses by his own labor was his property, man was king over his own property:

> [Property] in its particular application means "that dominion which one man claims and exercises over the external things of the world, in exclusion of every other individual."[91]

In other words, a man's house is his castle. To prevent the reoccurrence of the all—too—real invasions of houses through the vehicle of the general warrant in the colonial period, the Fourth Amendment requirement of a warrant to search property arises. If the government is going to invade man's private realm, it must have good reason to do so.

For the progressives, that good reason turns out to be the needs of the administrative state. The government has become big enough to help us, but it has also become big enough to hurt us. We have come full circle. In the pursuit of the goals of the administrative state, we have brought back the general warrant.

CONCLUSION

In this study I have shown how Fourth Amendment jurisprudence has changed since the Founding. For much of the twentieth century the amendment has been interpreted in a way that did not match the understanding of the Founders. In searches of public areas, for which the Founders did not require warrants, the modern judiciary decided warrants were necessary in order to protect the rights of people whom judges and other elites saw as misunderstood or as victims of modern capitalistic society.

Max Boot discusses this trend very effectively in his book, *Out of Order*. He cites many prominent judges and lawyers to elucidate this viewpoint. For example, Texas state judge Terry McDonald has said, "I look for the good in people,". . . the easy thing to do is send everyone to prison and disregard the fact that some crimes are committed by basically good people who deserve a second chance."[1] Another legal spokesperson, Catherine Richardson, president of the New York Bar Association has argued that,

> If we are ever to rid our society of crime, the war must be fought by addressing the root causes of crime—poverty, prejudice, injustice, alienation and fear. This is a battle that cannot be won by beefing up police, building more prisons or asking the judiciary to cave in to populist sentiments and abandon the rule of law.[2]

And Judge Lorin Duckman of New York emphasizes what he sees as a problem of racism:

> Judge Duckman was particularly perturbed by the parade of black defendants in his court. "Don't you understand that all you are do

ing is putting poor black men in jail?" he demanded of one assistant district attorney. When she replied, "Judge, I have a lot of poor black victims," Duckman flew off the handle. On another occasion, the judge told a prosecutor that he didn't understand "these people"—presumably meaning black defendants—because of his "middle-class background." The prosecutor in question happened to be black—unlike the judge.. . . Referring to one assault cause (sic) involving two African-American women, the judge proclaimed, "You know, sometimes certain things are just cultural."[3]

Criminals are not responsible for their behavior, but society is. Criminals are the victims; they are victims of a capitalistic, racist society. This view of criminals and society also affects Fourth Amendment cases, of course. For example, we find the judges in New York's First Department Appellate Division throwing out the search of a car that turned up a dead body because, they argued, when the police officer asked the suspect if he could search the car, he unduly intimidated the suspect:

> When a motorist, stopped for some minor traffic infraction on a lonely stretch of road in the dead of night, is approached by two imposing State Troopers—the very personification of State authority on the highway—one of whom leans over the car and asks, "Mind if we look in the trunk?" can the forthcoming affirmative response truly be regarded as the product of free will?[4]

In the state of New York, according to this decision, consent search is illegal, because there is no real consent. This decision overturned a murder conviction. We see how far the pendulum has swung towards the rights of criminals.

Finally, we have Judge Baer, a federal district court judge in New York City who made headlines when he excluded from court eighty pounds of cocaine and heroin as evidence. (He later overturned this decision under tremendous public pressure.) The officers in this case argued that they had probable cause to search a vehicle because they saw young men loading duffel bags into the trunk of a car in a known drug area. When the officers approached, the young men ran away. Judge Baer claimed their action was reasonable because in that area police were viewed as "corrupt, abusive, and violent." In fact, "Had the men not run away when the cops began to stare at them," the judge wrote, "it would have been unusual."[5]

I do not mean to claim, and certainly Boot does not claim, that all judges, or even a majority, perform as the ones mentioned above. Nor do I mean to claim that only judges have been influenced by the view of criminals and the criminal justice system just elaborated. Many other elites (politicians, bureaucrats, academics, and media elites) have accepted this view of criminals and the criminal justice system. Most judges do not go to the extremes that McDonald, Baer and Duckman do. But I do think these examples reveal the mindset of many in the judiciary, and many progressives in general. Criminals are seen as victims of society, so more of an attempt is made to protect the criminals. To quote Max Boot:

> The common problem, it seems to me, is that much of the judiciary is pursuing a fairly radical conception of justice. The courts are trying to provide a remedy for every conceivable "victim," and in the process, they hold no one accountable for his own conduct. In the world according to many of today's judges, plaintiffs deserve big payoffs because their injuries must have been somebody else's fault; criminals deserve understanding, not punishment, because their transgressions must be rooted in society's ills; and various "minorities"—whether a smelly panhandler kicked out of a public library or politicians kicked out of office by term limits – deserve protection from the vicissitudes of fortune.[6]

Because of racism and discrimination against the poor, these people had been given a raw deal, and it is the duty of judges to protect them. Judges came up with safeguards for these criminals. The Miranda warning is one. The exclusionary rule is another. A third protection is the one we have discussed, the warrant requirement for searches in public areas. To protect the poor and the powerless from the abuses of law enforcement, officers would now have to get a warrant before conducting a search. Unfortunately, in making this requirement modern judges forgot the warning of Pennsylvania Supreme Court Justice Tilghman concerning the danger to society of requiring warrants for searches and seizures in public areas ("But it is nowhere said, that there shall be no arrest without warrant. To have said so would have endangered the safety of society.")[7] The Founding generation realized that because of circumstances such as the mobility of suspects, to require warrants for searches in public areas was unwise. Clearly guilty individuals may go free. That is exactly what happened in the twentieth century with the combination of the warrant requirement for searches in public areas and the application of the exclusionary rule to illegal searches and seizures. When it comes to commercial searches, the modern judiciary has also rejected the Founder's understanding of the Fourth Amendment. As we have seen, the Founders realized the importance of private property and advocated strongly for warrants for the search of real property. Under the influence of progressives, modern judges and other elites have seen property and property holders as corrupt. Private property stood in the way of socializing government and the economy. This disrespect, amounting even to contempt, for property made it easier to justify invasions of property. Thus, in the twentieth century we first had the administrative search exception to the warrant clause that allowed for warrantless searches of business. Next we get the administrative search warrant, which requires a warrant but not probable cause, even though the Fourth Amendment specifically requires probable cause before a warrant can be issued. As I have pointed out, this is nothing more than the reappearance of the notorious general warrant that inspired the Fourth Amendment in the first place (The general warrant allowed British officers to search places without first demonstrating probable cause – see Chapter One). When it comes to businessmen, therefore, modern elites restrict their Fourth Amendment rights while enlarging the Fourth Amendment rights of criminals. It is a world turned upside down. At least when it comes to searches in public areas, the 1990s has seen a dramatic change in Fourth Amendment jurisprudence. The same cannot be said, however, for commercial searches.

Slowly but Surely a Return to First Principles? Searches in Public Areas in the 1990s

The United States Supreme Court appears to be returning to the original understanding of the amendment concerning searches in public areas. I say "appears" because the Court has not enunciated a principle that all searches in public areas will be based on probable cause. But, in the cases involving searches in public areas that have reached the Court, it has ruled that the reasonableness clause, not the warrant clause is controlling. We have already discussed *California v. Acevedo*[8], where the Court said a warrant was not needed to search a container in a car. In *Wyoming v. Houghton*,[9] Justice Scalia wrote the Opinion of the Court, in which he examined the history of the Fourth Amendment (see Chapters One through Three above), and argued that the Framers would have concluded that a warrantless search of containers in an automobile was reasonable. The Supreme Court ruled that officers could search a car passenger's belongings if there was probable cause:

> A passenger's personal belongings, just like the driver's belongings or containers attached to the car like a glove compartment, are "in" the car, and the officer has probable cause to search for contraband *in* the car.[10]

This emphasis on warrantless searches in public areas is more fully articulated in *Florida v. White.*[11] In *Florida* a vehicle was seized by the police officers as contraband. It was seized from a public street, and the officers conducted a warrantless inventory search. During the course of the search the officers discovered cocaine. The Florida Supreme Court ruled that absent exigent circumstances a search of an automobile required a warrant. The U. S. Supreme Court reversed. Justice Thomas, writing the Opinion of the Court, begins by noting that in interpreting the Fourth Amendment the Court has "taken care to inquire whether the action was regarded as an unlawful search and seizure at the time the Fourth Amendment was framed."[12] After examining the Founding-era laws (see Chapter Three above) and the automobile search case *Carroll v. United States* (267 U. S. 132; examined in Chapter Four above), Thomas says that, "The principles underlying the rule in *Carroll* and the Founding-era statutes upon which they are based fully support the conclusion that the warrantless seizure of respondent's car did not violate the Fourth Amendment."[13] Taking into consideration, as well, the 1991 decision in *California v. Acevedo* (and discussed in Chapter Five above), we see in the 1990s a partial return to the original understanding regarding searches in public areas. Each of these cases allows warrantless searches in public areas. In fact, I do not know one Supreme Court case of the 1990s that disallows a warrantless search in public areas. The tide has turned. Whether this is because the Court is responding to the increased concern about violent crime, or because twelve years of Republican presidents has brought about the appointment of five Supreme Court justices who, no matter what their differences on other issues,[14] are law—and-order justices, is uncertain. The return to the original understanding, even so, has not been complete. The Court, for example, has not overturned *Chadwick* (discussed in Chapter Five above), which disallowed warrantless probable cause searches of containers (outside automobiles) in public areas. It may be simply that the Court has not had a case yet involving such a search (it has not) and, by and large not being judicial activists, they prefer to decide cases narrowly, just deciding the particular issue before them. However, the trend is certainly moving back towards the Founders' original understanding of the Fourth Amendment in cases involving searches in public areas.

On the other hand, there has been no major commercial search case in the 1990s, and the law seems to be settled. The government can search without a warrant under the closely regulated business exception (which states that one consents to "reasonable forms government intrusion", like warrantless searches, when one enters what Congress deems to be a highly regulated industry) or with an administrative warrant, which, as I have shown, is no better than a general warrant. A good example of the settled state of the law occurred in 1996. Caterpillar Inc. underwent an inspection by the National Institute for Occupational Safety and Health (NIOSH), a part of the Department of Health and Human Services; because the United Auto Workers Union (UAW), representing workers in Caterpillar's York, Pennsylvania plant, claimed that the use of substances such as cadmium was causing health problems for workers. Caterpillar refused to allow an inspection of the plant, saying that it had provided NIOSH with extensive information, including documents explaining how the chemicals were being used and how the testing and monitoring of workers for exposure was being conducted. Furthermore, Caterpillar wanted NIOSH to establish limits, develop a methodology, and demonstrate probable cause for the inspection. NIOSH was twice granted a warrant (which, remember, does not require probable cause) for the inspection, and twice Caterpillar refused to honor the warrant.[15] A judge held Caterpillar in civil contempt and subjected it to fines. The company finally relented and permitted the inspection.[16] The business owners are therefore punished, or, more accurately, threatened with punishment, for exercising their constitutional rights. In the face of fines they are forced to relent to a search even though no probable cause has been demonstrated. They must accept the very same type of search that our Founders revolted against and that inspired the Fourth Amendment.

The Fourth Amendment: A Jurisprudence of Original Understanding

Justice would be better served by a return to the original understanding of the Fourth Amendment. Justice would be served in a twofold fashion. First, by allowing government to conduct warrantless searches in public areas based on probable cause (a trend, as we have seen, that has already started) guilty parties will be easier to find and convict. The guilty will be punished and the innocent will be protected. The cause of ordered liberty will be advanced by maintaining the distinction between liberty and license that we saw in Chapter 2 and that is so important to the success of self-government. Second, a Fourth Amendment jurisprudence of original understanding will protect the rights of commercial property owners. In Chapter 2, I discussed why the Founders were so concerned about protecting property rights. Private property serves the cause of justice by limiting government. There is a sphere of life that lies beyond, or is supposed to lie beyond, the touch of government. Protecting property rights necessarily limits the power of government; it helps to prevent tyranny. Private property is just that—private. Hence the warrant requirement. Government should not violate that private sphere unless it has good reason—unless it has probable cause. To ensure that the private sphere is protected from undue government interference the Founders preferred warrants for searches of property. Government officials would have to go to a neutral judge and demonstrate to his satisfaction that they had good reason—probable cause—to violate that separate, private sphere. To the degree that this process helps keep government in its rightful place, it protects all of us. Furthermore, according to the Declaration, among our natural rights is the right to liberty. Liberty, as I outlined in Chapter Two, includes the right to property. By protecting the rights of property owners, the natural rights of acquiring and maintaining property are protected.

This is one reason, as I have we shown, why the Progressives attacked property rights. Progressives deemed that the cause of justice could best be served by increasing the power of government enough to take care of everybody. In their view justice was best served not by limiting government, but by expanding it. All aspects of life, including commercial life, would have to come under governmental control. With the Progressive revolution in the twentieth century came the administrative state, which in turn brought about the devaluing of property rights. We see this in Fourth Amendment jurisprudence, with the advent of the administrative search warrant and the regulated industry exception to the warrant clause of the Fourth Amendment. A jurisprudence of original understanding, which acknowledges the importance of property in our politics and the natural rights of property owners, would return to a preference for a warrant in the search of commercial property. By a warrant I mean a warrant in the Fourth Amendment sense, one that must demonstrate probable cause. I use the word "preference" above because obviously in some cases exigent circumstances may argue against obtaining a warrant. For the most part, however, government should be able to search property only after it was able to convince a judge that it had probable cause to do so. This would protect the rights of commercial property owners, and more importantly, it would serve justice by returning our Fourth Amendment jurisprudence to its foundation upon the ideals of limited government and natural rights.

NOTES

INTRODUCTION

[1] Akhil Amar, "Fourth Amendment First Principles," *Harvard Law Review*, 107 (February 1994) 757-819.
[2] Jacob Landynski, *Search and Seizure: A Study in Constitutional Interpretation* (Baltimore: The Johns Hopkins Press, 1966), 42-48.
[3] John Dewey, *Individualism Old and New* (New York: Minton, Balch and Company, 1930), 72.
[4] John Dewey, *Liberalism and Social Action* (New York: G.P. Putnam's Sons, 1935), 89-90.
[5] *Wakely V. Hart*, 6 Binnery 316 [PA 1816], discussed in Chapter Three below.

CHAPTER 1

[1] John Adams, "Letter to William Tudor, 1817" in Bernard Schwartz, *The Bill of Rights: A Documentary History*. (New York: Chelsea House, 1971), 1:194.
[2] Nelson Lasson, *The History and Development of the Fourth Amendment to the United States Constitution* (Baltimore: The Johns Hopkins Press, 1937), 54.
[3] Telford Taylor, *Two Studies in Constitutional Interpretation* (Columbus, Ohio: Ohio University Press, 1969), 35.
[4] Nelson Lasson, 54.
[5] Schwartz, *The Bill of Rights: A Documentary History*, 186.
[6] Ibid., 190.
[7] Ibid., 199.
[8] Ibid., 200.
[9] Ibid., 202.
[10] Ibid., 205.

[11]*Marshall v. Barlow's, Inc.* 436 U.S. 307, 311 (1978).

[12]James Wilson, "Law Lectures" in *The Works of James Wilson*, ed. Robert Green McCloskey (Cambridge MA: Belknap Press, 1967), 2:588.

[13]Ibid., 588-9.

[14]Ibid., 589, emphasis in original.

[15]Ibid, 588.

[16]Daniel M. Harris, "The Return To Common Sense: A Response To 'The Incredible Shrinking Fourth Amendment," *American Criminal Law Review*, 22 (1984) 29.

[17]Ibid.; quoting Joseph Story, *Commentaries on the Constitution* (Boston: Hilliard Gray,1833),748.

[18]William Blackstone, *Commentaries on the Laws of England in Four Books*,(Philadelphia: J. B. Lippicott and Co, 1859), I:67.

[19]George Anastaplo, *The Constitution of 1787: A Commentary*, (Baltimore: The Johns Hopkins Press, 1989), 3-4.

[20]James R. Stoner, *Common Law and Liberal Theory: Coke, Hobbes, and the Origins of American Constitutionalism.* (Lawrence, KA: University Press of Kansas, 1992), 189.

[21]James Wilson, 2:334.

[22]Blackstone, I:138; The commentator Herbert Storing has argued that Blackstone left open what kind of right occupancy or possessions is, and in any case, since property is regulated by conventional laws, Blackstone is more concerned with those conventional laws. Herbert Storing, "William Blackstone" in *The History of Political Philosophy*, 2nd Ed., ed. Leo Strauss and Joseph Cropsey. (Chicago: The University of Chicago Press, 1972), 595-5

[23]Ibid, 40-42.

[24]Herbert Storing, 595, 603.

[25]Joseph Story, *A Familiar Exposition of the Constitution of the United States*. (North Shore IL: Regency Gateway, 1986), 36.

[26]Ibid., 38.

[27]Harris, 27.

[28]Ibid. 27-28.

[29]Ibid., 27.

[30]Ibid, 28-29.

[31]"The only true and natural foundations of society are the wants and fears of individuals." Blackstone, I:47.

CHAPTER 2

[1]Thomas G. West, *Vindicating the Founders: Race, Sex, Class, and Justice in the Origins of America* (Lanham, MD: Rowman and Littlefield Publishers, Inc., 1997), 39. Much of the material in this chapter is derived from West's chapter on property rights.

[2]Hamilton, "The Defense of the Funding System," in *Papers of Alexander Hamilton*, ed. Harold C. Syrett (New York: Columbia University Press, 1961-

79), 19:52; quoted in West, 38.

³*Vanhorne's Lessee v. Dorrance*, 2 Dallas 304, 310; quoted in West, 38.

⁴West, 39, quoting Edward J. Erler, "The Great Fence of Liberty: The Right of Property in the American Founding," in *Liberty, Property, and the Foundations of the American Constitution*, ed. Ellen F. Paul et al. (Albany N.Y.: State University of New York Press, 1988), 43.

⁵West, 63.

⁶1 New Hampshire Reports 266 (1818). For a discussion of this case see Chapter Three, pp. 55-59.

⁷95 Eng. Rep. 807 (K.B. 1765); quoted in *The Founders Constitution*, ed. by Philip B. Kurland and Ralph Lerner (Chicago: The University of Chicago Press, 1987), 5:234. Close is an ancient legal term that refers to land rightfully owned by a party; Steven H. Gifis, *Law Dictionary*, 3rd ed. (Hauppauge, NY: Barron's, 1991), 76.

⁸Alexander Hamilton, "The Farmer Refuted," *Selected Speeches and Writings of Alexander Hamilton*, ed. Morton J. Frisch (Washington, DC: American Enterprise Institute for Public Policy Research, 1985), 20; emphasis in original.

⁹James Wilson, "Law Lectures," in *The Works of James Wilson*, 2:587; emphasis added.

¹⁰ West, 161.

¹¹John Adams, *The Adams-Jefferson Letters*, ed. Lester J. Cappon (New York: Simon and Schuster, 1959), 551; quoted in West, 67.

¹²West, 160; 177.

13. 26 F. Cas. 832, 843-844 (C.C.D. Mass.); quoted in Bradford Wilson, "The Fourth Amendment as More Than a Form of Words: The View from the Founding," in *The Bill of Rights: Original Meaning and Current Understanding*. ed. Eugene W. Hickok, Jr. (Charlottesville, VA: The University Press of Virginia, 1991), 168.

¹⁴*Commonwealth v. Dana*, 43 Mass. (2 Met.) 329, 337 (1841); quoted in Bradford Wilson, 169.

¹⁵See the discussion of the *Apollon*, p. 48 below.

CHAPTER 3

¹Amar, 757-819.

²Ibid., 763.

³766-767; discussed on pp. 60-63 below.

⁴See p.60-61 below for a quotation from the relevant section of The Collections Act of 1789.

⁵Discussed on pp. 64-67 below.

⁶Emphasis added. This passage is quoted at length on p. 66 below.

⁷See Amar, 757-758 where he ridicules the Court's Fourth Amendment jurisprudence for its inconsistency. Also see Justice Scalia's concurring opinion in *California v. Acevedo* (111S.Ct. 1982, 1992 [1991]) in which Scalia criticizes twentieth century Supreme Court jurisprudence for rhetorically requiring

a warrant for all searches, even though the text of the Fourth Amendment does not support such a requirement, then creating some twenty exceptions to the warrant requirement.

[8] 267 U.S. 132 (1925). Discussed in Chapter Four below.

[9] Landynski, 90; the quotation from Black is taken from Forrest R. Black, "A Critique of the *Carroll* Case," Columbia Law Review, XXXIX (November, 1929): 1068, 1087.

[10] By early states I mean the original thirteen and Vermont. Vermont adopted a declaration of rights in 1777 that included a declaration against general warrants (Section 11). See Schwartz, *The Bill of Rights: A Documentary History*, 1:323; and Lasson, 82.

[11] Schwartz, *The Great Rights of Mankind: A History of the Bill of Rights*. (Madison, WI: Madison House, 1992), 90. Both Landynski (38) and Lasson (79-82) only mention seven states. Both forget Delaware, which passed a declaration of rights in 1776. Section 17 of that document condemns general warrants. See Schwartz, The Bill of Rights: A *Documentary History*, 1:278.

[12] 81, n.10. For example, the Massachusetts Declaration of Rights of 1780 (Part 1, Article 14), which is very close to the wording of the Fourth Amendment (see Landynski, 38 and Lasson, 82), states that "Every subject has a right to be secure from all unreasonable searches, and seizures of his person, his houses, his papers, and all his possessions. All warrants, *therefore*, are contrary to this right, if the cause or foundation of them be not previously supported by oath or affirmation; and if the order in the warrant to a civil officer, to make search in suspected places, or to arrest one or more suspected persons, or to seize their property, be not accompanied with a special designation of the persons or objects of search, arrest, or seizure: and no warrant ought to be issued but in cases, and with formalities, prescribed by the laws." Kurland and Lerner 5:237. Emphasis added.

[13] Kurland and Lerner, 5:237.

[14] [Samuel Bryan] "Centinel" I, in *Debates on the Constitution* ed. by Bernard Bailyn. (New York: The Library of America, 1993), 1:52-53.

[15] "Letters from the Federal Farmer, #4" in *Debates*, 1:279.

[16] In Bailyn, 1:872.

[17] Ibid., 2:538; 2:554; 2:560; 2:567.

[18] Robert A. Goldwin, "Congressman Madison Proposes Amendments to the Constitution," *The Framers and Fundamental Rights,* ed. Robert A. Licht (Washington, DC: AEI Press, 1991), 78.

[19] "The right of the people to be secure in their persons, houses, papers and effects, against unreasonable searches and seizures, shall not be violated, and no Warrants shall issue, but upon probable cause, supported by Oath or affirmation, and particularly describing the place to be searched, and the persons or things to be seized."

[20] Lasson, 100-103, explains how this happened. Congressman Benson, who was chairman of the committee appointed to arrange the amendments, made a motion on the House floor that the words "by warrants issuing" be

NOTES

stricken and replaced with the phrase "and no warrants shall issue." The House voted down this proposed change, but in committee afterwards Benson apparently substituted his own words for the House approved version. It is Benson's version that was later approved by the Senate and ratified by the states and is the Fourth Amendment of today. I can find no explanation from Benson or a contemporary for this change in the wording. Also see Kurland and Lerner, 5:237.

[21] See pp.50-60 below for some typical examples. Also, there were many federal cases involving customs laws. See Harris, 30-34.

[22] Taylor, 45.

[23] An Act for preventing an Illicit Trade and Intercourse between the Subjects of this State and the Enemy [Act of June 24, 1782], *New Jersey Statues At Large*, 287, 289, 293-294.

[24] An Act For an Impost on Goods, Wares and Merchandise Imported Into this State, [Passed 10 September 1778] *The Statues at Large of Pennsylvania* 252(Chapter 925); and An Act More Effectually to Prevent Illicit Trade With The Enemy, [passed 13 April 1782], *New York Statues at Large* 245(Chapter 39).

[25] Other examples of early state search and seizure laws include a state of Delaware law giving physicians the right to search ships for persons with contagious diseases, An Act to Prevent Infectious Diseases Being Brought into this State, and for other Purposes," (*The First Laws of the State of Delaware*, ed. John D. Cushing, vol. 2 of 2, part 2 of 2, (Wilmington, DE: Michael Glazier, Inc., 1981)1354-1358; and a North Carolina Law allowing warrantless inspections of ships, "An Act for Regulating the Pilotage and Facilitating the Navigation of Cape-Fear River," *The First Laws of the State of North Carolina*, ed. John D. Cushing, vol. 2 of 2, (Wilmington, DE: Michael Glazier, Inc., 1984)499-504.

[26] Lasson, 106.

[27] 3 Cranch, 448, 1806.

[28] 9 Wheat., 362, 1824.

[29] 7 Cranch, 339, 1813.

[30] Ibid., 367.

[31] Harris, 34; quoting *Little v. Barreme*, 2 Cranch 170, 176 (1804).

[32] Bradford Wilson, "The Fourth Amendment as More Than a Form of Words," 165. Notice many of the cases discussed in this chapter are trespass and (in the *Wakely* case) false imprisonment suits arising out of search and seizure actions. For a list of these early suits see Taylor, 188, notes 71 and 72.

[33] Ibid., 167-169.

[34] Taylor, 45. The 1914 case is *Weeks v. United States* (232 U.S. 383). In 1961 the Supreme Court, in *Mapp v. Ohio* (367 U.S. 643), applies the exclusionary rule to the states.

[35] *People v. DeFore*, 242 N.Y. 13 at 21 N.B. 585 (1926). For an excellent discussion of the remedial issue see Bradford Wilson, *Enforcing the Fourth Amendment: A Jurisprudential History* (New York: Garland, 1986).

NOTES

[36] 6 Binnery 316 [PA 1814].

[37] *Wakely*, 316.

[38] *Wakely*, 318; emphasis added.

[39] *Wakely*, 318-319. As mentioned in the previous chapter, it was at his peril because if the search did not turn up evidence, the person conducting the search could be sued for damages.

[40] *Wakely* does not mention officer justification, but obviously that is what the court means, for why else specify justification for private individuals only? For officer justification see *Rohan v. Sawin*, 59 Mass. 281, 284-285 (1850); *Reuck v. McGregor*, 32 NJL 70, 74 (1866); *Johnson v. State*, 30 GA 426, 430 (1860). The Georgia court in Johnson quotes no less than the famed English common law commentator Matthew Hale to back up its argument for officer justification for a warrantless arrest based on probable cause:
"by virtue of his office, empowered by law, to arrest felons, or those that are suspected of felony, and that before conviction and also before indictment. And these are under greater protection of the law, in execution of this part of their office, upon these two accounts:
"1. Because they are persons more eminently trusted by the law, as in many other incidents to their office, so in this.
"2. Because they are, by law, punishable, if they neglect their duty in it."
...these officers, that are thus entrusted, may without any other warrant but from themselves, arrest felons and those that are probably suspected of felonies." 2 Hale's Pleas of the Crown, 85, 86 and 1 East P. C. 301; quoted in *Johnson v. State*, 430-431.

[41] *Wakely*, 319, emphasis in original.

[42] 11 Johns. R. 500 (N.Y. 1814), 500.

[43] Ibid., 500.

[44] Ibid., 501.

[45] Ibid., 503.

[46] Ibid., 502.

[47] 1 New Hampshire Reports 266 (1818).

[48] Ibid., 266-267.

[49] Ibid., 271-272.

[50] Ibid., 272.

[51] Ibid., emphasis added.

[52] Ibid, 272-273.

[53] 72 Mass. (6 Gray) 435 (1856).

[54] Massachusetts statute 1855, c.215, section 13: quoted in *Jones v. Root*, 435.

[55] Collections Act, 1 Stat. 29, 43 (1789).

[56] The importance of the First Congress can not be over-emphasized. Its decisions have long been given special importance because it came into session a mere two years after the Constitutional Convention, because many of its members were delegates to the Constitutional Convention, and because it set the precedents for future Congresses. Indeed the Supreme Court has said,

"early congressional enactments 'provide 'contemporaneous and weighty evidence' of the Constitution's meaning.' Such 'contemporaneous legislative exposition of the Constitution . . . . , acquiesced in for a long term of years, fixes the construction to be given its provisions.'" *Printz v. United States* (117 S. Ct. 2367, 1997) (quoting *Bowsher v. Synar*, 478 U.S. 714, 723-724 (1986) and *Marsh v. Chambers*, 463 U.S. 783, 790 (1983), and *Myers v. United States*, 272 U. S. 52, 175 (1926)).

[57] James Etienne Viator, "The Fourth Amendment in the Nineteenth Century," in Hickok, 175.

[58] Ibid.

[59] Also see Harris, 29; Lasson, 125-126.

[60] 1 Stat. 199, 207.

[61] Section 32 of the Act reads as follows: "And for the better discovery of any such spirits so fraudulently deposited, hid or concealed, it shall be lawful for any judge of any court of the United States . . . .. upon reasonable cause of suspicion, to be made out to the satisfaction of such judge or justice, by the oath or affirmation of and person or persons, by special warrant or warrants under their respective hands and seals, to authorize any of the officers of inspection, by day, in the presence of a constable or other officer of the peace, to enter into all and every such place or places in which any of the said spirits shall be suspected to be so fraudulently deposited, hid or concealed, and to seize and carry away any of the said spirits. " Ibid.

[62] An Act Further to Provide for the Collection of Duties, 3 Stat. 231, 232 (1815).

[63] Ibid.

[64] Ibid., emphasis in original.

[65] For further example of acts that differentiate between searches on one's premises and outside of those premises, see An Act to Provide more Effectually for the Collection of Merchandise Imported into the United States and of the Duties Imposed by Law on Goods, Wares and on Tonnage of Ships or Vessels (1 Stat. 145, sections 48 and 51) and Duty Collection Act (1 Stat. 627, sections 66-70). Cf. An Act to Reduce Internal Taxation and to Amend an Act Entitled An Act to Provide Internal Revenue to Support the Government, to Pay Interest on the Public Debt and for other Purposes (14 Stat. 98, section 15; which requires a revenue officer to obtain a search warrant before searching premises that are being used to commit fraud on the United States) with An Act for Enrolling and Licensing Ships or Vessels to be Employed in the Coasting Trade, and Fisheries, and for Regulating the Same (1 Stat. 305, section 27, which allows the officer to search any ship or vessel without a warrant). Other examples of acts that require warrants to search premises are: An Act to Regulate the Disposition of the Proceeds of Fines, Penalties, and Forfeitures Incurred under Laws Relating to the Customs and for other Purposes (14 Stat. 546), An Act to Amend Section Three-thousand and Sixty-six of the Revised Statutes of the United States, in Relation to the Authority of Search Warrants (22 Stat. 49), the Act of 20 February 1865 (13 Stat. 441, Sec. 3), and the Act of 10 February

1891 (26 Stat. 742, Sec. 5).

CHAPTER 4

[1] Joseph D. Gano, "Rethinking the Fourth Amendment Warrant Requirement," *American Criminal Law Review* 19 (Winter 1982) 630-631.

[2] Ibid., 605

[3] 428 U.S. 364 (1976). Gano is writing before *Ross*, when police had much less leeway in searching vehicles without a warrant.

[4] Gano, 649-650.

[5] Ibid., 650; emphasis in the original.

[6] The "plain view" doctrine state that officers may seize contraband in plain view, even if they do not have a warrant, or if they do have a warrant, even if the item are not listed in the warrant if it is apparent that the item is subject to seizure. See *Washington v. Chrisman*, 455 U. S. 1 (1982), allowing the warrantless seizure of marijuana seeds and a pipe from a dorm room which were in plain view of an officer legally in the room.

[7] 267 U S 132.

[8] Ibid., 134.

[9] It seems that Detroit was a major point of entry for prohibited liquor, with smugglers often traveling across the border from Detroit to Windsor, Ontario, Canada to procure liquor. See ibid., 160.

[10] *Carroll*, 134-136.

[11] Ibid., 143.

[12] Ibid.

[13] Quoted in ibid.

[14] Quoted in ibid., 144.

[15] *Congressional Record*, 67th Cong., 1st session, 1921, 61, pt. 6, 5632.

[16] Ibid.,5637.

[17] Ibid., 5565.

[18] Ibid., 5565-5566.

[19] Ibid., 5566.

[20] Ibid., pt. 8: 7891.

[21] Ibid., pt.6:5566.

[22] Ibid., 5564.

[23] Ibid., pt. 8: 7663.

[24] Ibid., 7850.

[25] Ibid.

[26] *Carroll*, 147.

[27] Ibid.,147-149.

[28] Ibid., 149 emphasis added.

[29] Ibid., 150-153.

[30] Ibid., 153, emphasis added.

[31] A criticism of the Court's reasoning is that it limits its discussion to laws and does not consider court cases in its discussion of the history of the development of the Fourth Amendment, perhaps because of the scarcity of cases in-

volving search and seizure, especially on the federal level, in the nineteenth century, as was discussed in Chapter 3.

[32] *Carroll*, 153-154.
[33] Ibid., 155-156.
[34] Ibid., 160-162.
[35] Landynski, 90—91; emphasis added.
[36] 338 US 160 (1949).
[37] The violation occurred in 1947. Although national prohibition had been lifted by then, Oklahoma was a "dry" state.
[38] *Brinegar*, 160-165.
[39] Ibid., 176-178.
[40] Ibid., 175—176.
[41] See Chapter Six below for a further explanation of the Progressive revolution (of which the New Deal was a part) in political and judicial thought.
[42] *United States v. Di Re*, 332 U. S. 581 (1948).
[43] Landynski, 92-93.
[44] See discussion in Chapter Three of *Wakely v. Hart* and *The Apollon*. Also see Harris, 30-34.

CHAPTER 5

[1] 433 U. S. 1 (1977).
[2] Ibid, 3.
[3] Ibid., 3-5.
[4] See *Chimel v. California*, 395 U.S. 752, 762-763 (1969).
[5] *Chadwick*, 6; quoting the court of appeals decision, 532 F. 2d 773, 781 (1976).
[6] Ibid., 7. Opinion of the Court paraphrasing the federal government's argument.
[7] Ibid., quoting *Katz v. United States*, 389 U.S. 347, 351 (1967).
[8] Ibid., 8-9. Modern legal scholars make a related point. Carol S. Steiker ("Second Thoughts About First Principles," *Harvard Law Review*, 107 [February 1994] 824), for example, argues that whatever the original understanding was, warrants are needed for searches in public areas because of the nature of modern law enforcement:

> ...at the time of the drafting and ratifying of the Fourth Amendment, nothing even remotely resembling modern law enforcement existed. The invention in the nineteenth century of armed, quasi-military, professional police forces, whose form, function, and daily presence differ dramatically from that of the colonial constabulary, requires that modern-day judges and scholars rethink both the relationship between "reasonableness" and "warrants" and the nature of Fourth Amendment remedies.

Similar sentiments are expressed by Silas J. Wasserstrom and Louis Michael Seidman ("The Fourth Amendment as Constitutional Theory," The *Georgetown Law Journal*, 77[October 1988], 82-84.).
    [9]Ibid., 8-11.
    [10]417 U.S. 583, 590.
    [11]*Chadwick*, 12.
    [12]Ibid., 13.
    [13]*Chadwick*, 23.
    [14]Ibid., 22-23.
    [15]442 U.S. 753 (1979).
    [16]Ibid., 755-756.
    [17]Ibid., 762—763.
    [18]Craig M. Bradley, "Two Models of the Fourth Amendment," *Michigan Law Review* 83 (May 1985) 1468.
    [19]456 U.S. 798 (1982).
    [20]Ibid., 823, 825.
    [21]111 S. Ct. 1982 (1991).
    [22]Ibid., 1988.
    [23]Ibid., 1991.
    [24]Ibid.
    [25]Ibid., 1988.
    [26]Ibid., 1989-1990.
    [27]Ibid., 1991.
    [28]Ibid.
    [29]Ibid.
    [30]Ibid., 1992.
    [31]Ibid.
    [32]Ibid., 1993.
    [33]Ibid.
    [34]Ibid., 1994. Emphasis added.
    [35]383 U.S. 413, 424-433.
    [36]Ibid., 426.
    [37]Ibid.
    [38]Ibid., 431-432.
    [39]I draw the reader's attention to the increasing demand among elites, including some conservatives, to legalize drugs.

CHAPTER 6

[1]Carlos B. Castillo, "Discord Among Federal Courts of Appeals: The Constitutionality of Warrantless Searches of Employers' OSHA Records." *University of Miami Law Review*, 45 (September 1990) 201-202.
    [2]Silas J. Wasserstrom and Louis Michael Seidman, "The Fourth Amendment as Constitutional Theory." *The Georgetown Law Journal* 77 (October 1988) 27.

[3] Representative cases are: *McDonald v. U.S.* (335 U.S. 451, 1948), *Chimel v. California* (395 U.S. 752, 1969), *Payton v. New York* (445 U.S. 573, 1980).
[4] Lasson, 124.
[5] Ibid.
[6] 327 U.S. 186.
[7] Ibid., 188.
[8] Federal Fair Labor Standards Act 52 Stat. 1060. Quoted in ibid., 198-199.
[9] *Congressional Record*, 75th Cong., 2nd session, 1937, 82, pt. 2, 1480.
[10] *Congressional Record*, 75th Cong., 1st session, 1937, 81, pt.7, 7743-7744.
[11] *Congressional Record*, 75th Cong., 2nd session, 1937, 82, pt. 2, 1484.
[12] *Congressional Record*, 75th Cong., 3rd session, 1938, 83, pt. 7, 7420.
[13] Ibid., 7395.
[14] *Oklahoma Press Publishing Co.*, 192.
[15] Ibid., 188.
[16] Ibid.
[17] Ibid., 218, 192, 214.
[18] Ibid., 204.
[19] Ibid., 204-205.
[20] *Silverthorne Lumber Company, Inc., Et Al v. United States*, 251 U. S. 385 (1920).
[21] *Wilson v. U.S.*, 221 U.S. 361.
[22] *Oklahoma Press Publishing Co.*, 205-206.
[23] Ibid., 207.
[24] Ibid., 208.
[25] Ibid., 208-209.
[26] Ibid., 218. The quotation is from the Declaration of Independence.
[27] One measure of the scope of administrative law is the size of the Federal Register. The Register publishes rules and regulations that are made by federal administrative agencies. In 1993 the Federal Register was 69,608 pages long. See Craig E. Richardson and Geoff C. Ziebert, *Strangled by Red Tape: A Heritage Foundation Collection of Regulatory Horror Stories* (Washington D. C.: The Heritage Foundation, 1995) 11.
[28] *Oklahoma Press Publishing Co.*, 219.
[29] Ibid., 195.
[30] 328 U. S. 582.
[31] In his dissent Justice Rutledge was particularly upset that the Court allowed this aspect of the search:
the situation was such that his (the officer that flashed his light into the window of the inside office) action clearly created in Davis's mind the impression that he either was entering by force or intended to do so....whatever may be the scope of search incident to lawful arrest for a misdemeanor, I know of no decision which goes so far as to rule that this right of search extends to breaking and entering locked premises by force. (Ibid., 623).

NOTES

[32] Ibid., 585-587.
[33] Ibid., 588.
[34] Ibid., 591.
[35] Ibid., 593-594.
[36] Scott Bullock, "Is Your Home a Castle? Not if You're a Renter." *The Wall Street Journal*, Wednesday, January 3, 1996, A9.
[37] *Davis*, 596-597.
[38] Ibid., 616-618. Many of these laws were discussed in Chapter Three.
[39] Ibid., 609.
[40] Ibid., 602.
[41] Ibid., emphasis added.
[42] Ibid., 594-595.
[43] The New Deal justices are the Supreme Court appointees of President Franklin Roosevelt (1933-1945) Roosevelt appointed nine justices to the court in the twelve years of his presidency. Among the justices he appointed were, William Douglas, Hugo Black, Robert Jackson, Harlan Stone, Felix Frankfurter, Stanley Reed, Frank Murphy and Wiley Rutledge.
[44] Herbert Croly, *The Promise of American Life*, (New York: The MacMillan Company, 1909) 209. Emphasis added.
[45] Ibid., 214.
[46] Ibid, 209.
[47] Ibid., 382.
[48] Ibid.
[49] Ibid., 383.
[50] John Dewey, "Philosophies of Freedom," in *Philosophy and Civilization* (New York: Minton, Balch and Company, 1931), 281.
[51] John Dewey, *The Public and its Problems* (New York: Henry Holt and Co., 1927), 34.
[52] John Dewey, *Individualism Old and New*, 72.
[53] John Dewey, *Liberalism and Social Action*, 89-90.
[54] John Dewey, *The Public and Its Problems*, 169-170. For an excellent discussion of Dewey's political views see James H. Nichols, Jr., "Pragmatism and the U. S. Constitution," in *Confronting the Constitution*, ed. Allan Bloom (Washington, DC: The AEI Press, 1990), 368-388.
[55] Thomas G. West, *Vindicating the Founders*, 59.
[56] Donald R. Brand, *Corporatism and the Rule of Law: A Study of the National Recovery Administration* (Ithaca, NY: Cornell University Press, 1988), 70.
[57] Ibid., 54-55.
[58] Thomas G. West, *Vindicating the Founders*, 58.
[59] Ibid.

CHAPTER 7

[1] See pp. 165-168 below.

[2] 387 U. S. 523 (1967).
[3] James B. Haddad, "Well-Delineated Exceptions, Claims of Sham, and Fourfold Probable Cause," *The Journal of Criminal Law and Criminology* 68(June 1977) 221.
[4] Thomas G. West, *Vindicating The Founders*, 55.
[5] 387 U.S. 541 (1967).
[6] *See v. City of Seattle*, 387 U.S. 541, 541-542.
[7] Ibid., 543.
[8] See above, pp.131-132.
[9] *See v. City of Seattle*, 544-545.
[10] Ibid., 545.
[11] *Camera*, 535.
[12] Ibid., 537.
[13] 359 U.S. 360.
[14] *Camera*, 538; quoting *Frank v. Maryland*, Justice Douglas dissenting, 359, U.S.,383.
[15] Ibid., 539; citing *Oklahoma Press Pub. Co.*
[16] Susan M. McDonough, "The Fourth Power? Administrative Searches vs. The Fourth Amendment," *New England Journal of Criminal and Civil Confinement* 20 (Winter 1993) 231.
[17] U. S. Constitution, Amendment IV.
[18] Wasserstrom and Seidman, 33.
[19] See pp. 165-168 below.
[20] 397 U.S. 72 (1970).
[21] Earlier a federal agent had attended a party catered by Colonnade and noticed a possible violation. *Colonnade*, 397 U.S. 72, 72-73.
[22] 26 U.S. Code, Section 5146 (b); quoted in ibid., 73.
[23] 26 U. S. Code, Section 7342; quoted. in ibid., 74.
[24] *Colonnade*, 74.
[25] Ibid., 76.
[26] Ibid., 75-77; especially note 9.
[27] *See v. City of Seattle;* quoted in ibid., at 76.
[28] I am indebted to Thomas West for this insight.
[29] 406 U. S. 311.
[30] *Biswell*, 311-312.
[31] Ibid., 312-313.
[32] Ibid., 315.
[33] John Wesley Hall, Jr., *Search and Seizure*, 2nd ed., vol. 2 of 2 (New York: Clark Boardman Callaghan) 1993, 385.
[34] Ibid., 392.
[35] Ibid., 385. See the discussion *of New York v. Burger*, 185-192 below.
[36] Ibid., 392.
[37] Ibid., 402.
[38] Steven T. Wax, "The Fourth Amendment, Administrative Searches and the Loss of Liberty," *Environmental Law*, 18 (1988) 920; quoting *Biswell*, 317.

[39] 406 U.S. 311, 315.

[40] Eileen Dribin, "Constitutional Law: Fourth Amendment—Search and Seizure—Carefully Defined Warrantless Administrative Inspections Are Permitted Under Federal Gun Control Act of 1968. *United States v. Biswell*, 406 U. S. 311 (1972)." (Casenotes) *Catholic University Law Review* 22 (1973) 501.

[41] Ibid., 502.
[42] 429 U. S. 338 (1977).
[43] 436 U.S. 307 (1978).
[44] *G. M. Leasing Corp.*, 351.
[45] 18 Howard 272.
[46] *G. M. Leasing Corp.*, 353, emphasis added.
[47] Ibid.
[48] Ibid., 354.
[49] Ibid.
[50] 1 Annals of Congress 438; quoted in ibid, 355.
[51] *G.M. Leasing Corp.*, 355.
[52] 26 U. S. Code section 6331 (b); see ibid., 356.
[53] Ibid., 358; quoting *Camera*, 528-529.
[54] 29 U. S. C., Section 657 (a).
[55] *Barlow's* 309.
[56] Ibid., 309-310.
[57] Ibid., 310.
[58] Ibid., 311.
[59] See Chapter One.
[60] *Barlow's*, 311.
[61] Ibid., 313.
[62] Ibid., 313-314.
[63] Ibid., 315.
[64] Ibid., 316.
[65] Ibid., 316-320.
[66] Ibid., 320-321; emphasis added.
[67] 452 U.S. 594 (1981).
[68] 482 U.S. 691 (1987).
[69] *Dewey*, 596-597.
[70] Ibid., 597-598.
[71] Ibid., 602-603.

[72] Remember that one of the justifications for warrantless searches of businesses mentioned earlier in this chapter is that there is a long history of extensive government regulation of those businesses and therefore anybody that opens a business in that particular industry, e.g., liquor, de facto consents to the extensive regulation, including warrantless searches. See,159-168 above and *Dewey*,(610-612).

[73] *Dewey*, 612.
[74] Hall, 386.
[75] *Dewey*, 613-614.

NOTES

[76]Wax, 922.

[77]The police book is where junkyard operators record the automobiles and vehicle parts in their possession. (*Burger*, 694-5).

[78]Ibid., 694, and note 1.
[79]Ibid., 699-702.
[80]Ibid., 702-703.
[81]Hall, 390.
[82]*Burger*, 705.
[83]Ibid., 708-711.
[84]Ibid., 711.
[85]Ibid., 718.
[86]Ibid., 720-721.
[87]Ibid., 724-727. The Court's argument can be found at 712-718.
[88]Ibid., 728.
[89]Ibid., 729.

[90]John Dickinson, "Letter 7," *Letters From a Farmer*, in *The Political Writing of John Dickinson, 1764-1774*, ed. Paul L. Ford (New York: Da Capo, 1970) 356.

[91]James Madison, "Essay on Property," in *The Writings of James Madison*, ed. Gaillard Hunt, 9 vols. (New York: G.P. Putnam's Sons, 1906), vol. 6:101.

CONCLUSION

[1]Max Boot, *Out of Order: Arrogance, Corruption, and Incompetence on the Bench* (New York: Basic Books, 1998), 32. [2]Quoted in ibid., 35.

[3]Boot, 44-45.
[4]Quoted in Ibid., 75.
[5]Quoted in ibid., 86.
[6]Ibid., 199-200.
[7]*Wakely*, 318.
[8]See discussion of *Acevedo*, pp. 110-116 above.
[9]119 S. Ct. 1297 (1999).
[10]Ibid., 1301.
[11]119 S. Ct. 1555 (1999).
[12]Ibid., 1558.
[13]Ibid., 1559.

[14]The Court has decided many cases in controversial areas by a 5-4 vote in recent years (Federalism, Commerce Clause, First Amendment, Affirmative Action and Equal Protection) by a 5-4 vote in recent years. However in the area of criminal justice (including Fourth Amendment, the majority on the Court is much larger, sometimes unanimous or approaching unanimity.

[15]Frederick Rose, *The Wall Street Journal*, 22 April 1996, B6.

[16]Susan Carey, *The Wall Street Journal*, 6 May 1996, A8.

BIBLIOGRAPHY

Articles and Books

Amar, Akhil Reed. "Fourth Amendment First Principles." *Harvard Law Review.* 107 (February 1994): 757-819.

Anastaplo, George. *The Constitution of 1787: A Commentary.* Baltimore: The John Hopkins University Press, 1989.

Bailyn, Bernard, ed. *Debates on the Constitution.* 2 vols. New York: The Library of America, 1993.

Blackstone, William. *Commentaries on the Laws of England in Four Books.* Philadelphia: J. B. Lippicott and Co., 1859.

Boot, Max. *Out of Order: Arrogance, Corruption, and Incompetence on the Bench.* New York: Basic Books, 1998.

Bradley, Craig M. "Two Models of the Fourth Amendment." *Michigan Law Review* 83 (May 1985): 1468-1501.

Brand, Donald R. *Corporatism and the Rule of Law: A Study of the National Recovery Administration.* Ithaca, NY: Cornell University Press, 1988.

Bullock, Scott. "Is Your Home a Castle? Not if You're a Renter." *Wall Street Journal,* 3 January 1999, (A).

Carey, Susan. "Caterpillar to Face Fines if Inspectors Not Allowed Entry." *Wall Street Journal,* 6 May 1996, 8(A).

Castillo, Carlos B., "Discord Among Federal Courts of Appeals: The Constitutionality of Warrantless Searches of Employers' OSHA Records." *University Of Miami Law Review,* 45 (September 1990):201-241.

Croly, Herbert. *The Promise of American Life.* New York: The MacMillan Company, 1909.

Cushing, John D., comp., *The First Laws of the State of Delaware.* 2

vols. Wilmington, DE: Michael Glazier, Inc., 1981.

--------., comp., *The First Laws of the State of North Carolina.* 2 vols. Wilmington, DE: Michael Glazier Inc., 1984.

Dewey, John. *Individualism Old and New.* New York: Minton, Balch and Company, 1930.

--------. *Liberalism and Social Action.* New York: G. P. Putnam's Sons, 1935.

--------. "Philosophies of Freedom." In *Philosophy and Civilization.* New York: Minton, Balch and Company, 1931.

--------. *The Public and its Problems.* New York: Henry Holt and Co., 1927.

Dickinson, John. "Letter # 7," *Letters From a Farmer.* In *Political Writings of John Dickinson*, ed. Paul L. Ford. New York: Da Capo, 1970.

Dribin, Eileen. "Casenote." *Catholic University Law Review* 22 (Winter 1973): 496-502.

Gano, Joseph D. "Rethinking the Fourth Amendment Warrant Requirement." *American Criminal Law Review* 19 (Winter 1982): 603-650.

Gifis, Steven H. *Law Dictionary.* Hauppauge, NY: Barron's 1991.

Goldwin, Robert A. "Congressman Madison Proposes Amendments to the Constitution." In *The Framers and Fundamental Rights*, ed. Robert A. Licht. Washington, DC: AEI Press, 1991.

Haddad, James B. "Well-Delineated Exceptions, Claims of Sham, and Fourfold Probable Cause." *Journal of Criminal Law and Criminology* 68 (June 1977):198-225.

Hall, John Wesley, Jr. *Search and Seizure.* 2nd ed. 2 vols. Deerfield, IL: Clark, Boardman, Callaghan, 1993.

Hamilton, Alexander. "The Farmer Refuted." In *Selected Speeches and Writings of Alexander Hamilton*, ed. Morton J. Frisch. Washington, DC: American Enterprise Institute for Public Policy Research, 1985.

Harris, Daniel M. "The Return to Common Sense: A Response to 'The Incredible Shrinking Fourth Amendment.'" *American Criminal Law Review* 22(Summer 1984): 25-47.

Kurland, Phillip B. and Ralph Lerner, eds. *The Founder's Constitution.* 5 vols. Chicago: University of Chicago Press, 1987.

Lasson, Nelson B. *The History and Development of the Fourth Amendment to the United States Constitution.* Baltimore: The Johns Hopkins Press, 1937.

Landynski, Jacob W. *Search and Seizure and the* Supreme Court: A

Study in Constitutional *Interpretation*. Baltimore: The Johns Hopkins Press, 1966.

Madison, James. "Essay on Property." In *The Writings of James Madison*, ed. Gaillard Hunt. 9 vols. New York: G. P. Putnam's Sons, 1906.

McDonough, Susan M. "The Fourth Power? Administrative Searches vs. The Fourth Amendment." *New England Journal of Criminal and Civil Confinement* 20 (Winter 1993):195-237.

Nichols, James H., Jr. "Pragmatism and the U. S. Constitution." In *Confronting the Constitution: The Challenge to Locke, Montesquieu, Jefferson, and the Federalists From Utilitarianism, Historicism, Marxism, Freudianism, Pragmatism Existentialism....* ed. Allan Bloom. Washington, DC: The AEI Press, 1990.

Richardson, Craig E., and Geoff C. Ziebert. *Strangled by Red Tape: The Heritage Foundation Collection of Regulatory Horror Stories*. Washington, DC: The Heritage Foundation, 1995.

Rose, Frederick. "Caterpillar Again Blocks Inspection by Government of Parts-Making Plant." *Wall Street Journal*, 22 April 1996, 6(B).

Schwartz, Bernard. *The Bill of Rights: A Documentary History*. 2 vols. New York: Chelsea House, 1971.

--------. *The Great Rights of Mankind: A History of the American Bill of Rights*. Madison WI: Madison House, 1992.

Steiker, Carol S. "Second Thoughts About First Principles." *Harvard Law Review* 107 (February1994): 820-857.

Stoner, James R. *Common Law and Liberal Theory: Coke, Hobbes, and the Origins of American Constitutionalism*. Lawrence, Kansas: University Press of Kansas, 1992.

Storing Herbert J. "William Blackstone" in *The History of Political Philosophy*. ed. Leo Strauss and Joseph Cropsey. 2nd ed. Chicago: The University of Chicago Press, 1972.

Story, Joseph. *Commentaries on the Constitution of the United States*. 1st ed. 3 vols. Boston: Hilliard, Gray, 1833.

-------. *A Familiar Exposition of the Constitution of the United States*. North Shore, IL: Regnery Gateway, 1986.

Taylor, Telford. *Two Studies in Constitutional Interpretation*. Columbus, OH: Ohio University Press, 1969.

Viator, James Etienne. "The Fourth Amendment in the Nineteenth Century." In *The Bill of Rights: Original Meaning and Current Understanding*, ed. Eugene W. Hickok, Jr., 172-183. Charlottesville, VA: University Press of Virginia, 1991.

Wasserstrom, Silas J. and Louis Michael Seidman. "The Fourth

Amendment as Constitutional Theory." *The Georgetown Law Journal* 77 (October 1988): 19-112.
Wax, Steven T. "The Fourth Amendment, Administrative Searches and the Loss of Liberty." *Environmental Law* 18 (1988):911-930.
West, Thomas G. *Vindicating the Founders: Race, Sex, Class, and Justice in the Origins of America*. Lanham, MD: Rowman and Littlefield, 1997.
Wilson, Bradford. *Enforcing the Fourth Amendment: A Jurisprudential History*. New York: Garland, 1986.
--------. "The Fourth Amendment as More Than a Form of Words: The View from the Founding." In *The Bill of Rights: Original Meaning and Current Understanding*, ed. Eugene W. Hickok, Jr., 151-171. Charlottesville, VA: University Press of Virginia, 1991.
Wilson, James. *The Works of James Wilson*, ed. Robert Green McCloskey. 2 vols. Cambridge, MA: Belknap Press, 1967.

COURT CASES

The Apollon, 22 U. S. 362 (1824).
Arkansas v. Sanders, 442 U. S. 616 (1979).
Brinegar v. United States, 338 U. S. 160 (1949).
Burford, Ex Parte, 3 Cranch 448 (1805).
California v. Acevedo, 111 S. Ct. 1982 (1991).
Camera v. Municipal Court, 387 U. S. 523 (1967).
Carroll v. United States, 267 U. S. (1925).
Chimel v. California, 395 U. S. 752 (1969).
Colonnade v. United States, 397 U. S. 72 (1970).
Davis v. United States, 328 U. S. 582 (1946).
Donovan v. Dewey, 452 U. S. 594 (1981).
Florida v. White, 119 S. Ct. 1555 (1999).
Frank v. Maryland, 359 U. S. 360 (1959).
G. M. Leasing v. United States, 429 U. S. 338 (1977).
Illinios v. Lidster, 02-1060 (2004).
Indianapolis v. Edmond, 531 U. S. 32 (2000)
Johnson v. State, 30 GA 426 (1860).
Jones v. Root, 72 Mass. (6 Grey) 435 (1856).
Jones v. Gibson, 1 N. H. Reports 266 (1818).
Katz v. United States, 389 U. S. 347 (1967).
Locke V. United States, 7 Cranch 339 (1813).
Mapp v. Ohio, 367 U. S. 643 (1961).
McDonald v. United States, 335 U. S. 451 (1948).

Marshall v. Barlow's, Inc., 436 U. S. 307 (1978).
Memoirs v. Massachusetts, 383 U.S. 413 (1966).
Murray's Lessee v. Hoboken Land Co., 18 Howard 272 1856).
New York v. Burger, 482 U. S. 691 (1987).
Oklahoma Press v. Walling, 327 U. S. 186 (1946).
Payton v. New York, 445 U. S. 573 (1980).
People v. Defore, 242 N. Y. 13 at 21 N. B. 585 (1926).
Printz v. United States, 117 S. Ct. 2365 (1997).
Reuck v. McGregor, 32 NJL 70 (1866).
Rohan v. Sawin, 59 Mass 281 (1850).
Sailly v. Smith, 11 Johns R. 500 (N. Y. 1814).
See v. City of Seattle, 387 U.S. 541 (1967).
Silverthorne v. United States, 251 U. S. 385 (1920).
South Dakota v. Opperman, 428 U. S. 364 (1976).
United States v. Biswell, 406 U. S. 31 (1972).
United States v. Chadwick, 433 U. S. 1 (1977).
United States v. Di Re, 332 U. S. 581 (1948).
United States v. Ross, 456 U. S. 798 (1982).
Wakely v. Hart, 6 Binney 316 (PA 1814).
Washington v. Chrisman, 455 U. S. 1 (1982).
Wilson v. United States, 221 U. S. 361 (1911).
Wyoming v. Houghton, 119 S.Ct. 1297 (1999).

STATUTES

Act of 10 February 1891. 26 Statutes at Large 742.
Act of 20 February 1865. 13 Statutes at Large 441.
An Act For an Impost on Goods, Wares and Merchandise Imported Into this State. The Statutes at Large of Pennsylvania, 252 (1778).
An Act for preventing an Illicit Trade and Intercourse *Between the Subjects of this State and the Enemy. New Jersey Statutes at Large 287* (1782).
An Act More Effectually to Prevent Illicit Trade With The Enemy. New York Statutes at Large 245 (1782).
An Act Further to Provide for the Collection of *Duties. 3 Statutes at Large 231* (1815).
An Act Repealing Duties. 1 Statutes at Large 199 (1791).
An Act to Amend Section Three-thousand and Sixty-six of the Revised Statutes of the United States, in Relation to the Authority of Search Warrants. 22 Statutes at Large 49 (1882).

An Act for Enrolling and Licensing Ships or Vessels to be Employed in the Coasting Trade, and Fisheries, and for Regulating the Same. 1 Statutes at Large 305 (1793)
An Act to Provide for the Establishment of Fair Labor Standards in Employments in and Affecting Interstate Commerce, and for Other Purposes. 52 Statutes at Large 1060 (1938).
An Act to Provide more Effectually for the Collection of Merchandise Imported into the United States and of the Duties Imposed by Law on Goods, Wares and on Tonnage of Ships or Vessels. 1 Statutes at Large 145 (1790).
An Act to Reduce Internal Taxation and to Amend an Act Entitled "An Act to Provide Internal Revenue to Support the Government, to Pay Interest on the Public Debt and for other Purposes" Approved June Thirteenth Eighteen Hundred and Sixty-four and Acts Thereof. 14 Statutes at Large 98 (1866).
An Act to Regulate the Disposition of the Proceeds of Fines, Penalties, and Forfeitures Incurred under Laws Relating to the Customs and for other Purposes. 14 Statutes at Large 546 (1867).
The Collections Act. 1 Statutes at Large 29 (1789).
Duty Collection Act. 1 Statutes at Large 627 (1799).
Excise Tax Technical Change Act. U. S. Code. Vol. 26, Sec. 5146(b) (1958).
Internal Revenue Code. U. S. Code. Vol. 26 Sec. 7342 (1958).
Internal Revenue Code of 1954. U.S. Code. Vol. 26 Sec. 6331 (b).
Occupational Safety and Health Act. U. S. Code. Vol. 29, Sec. 657(a) (1970).

GOVERNMENT DOCUMENTS

Congressional Record, 67th Congress, 61, pt.6, 1st Session, 1921.
Congressional Record, 67th Congress, 61, pt. 8, 1st Session, 1921.
Congressional Record, 75th Congress, 81, pt. 7, 1st Session, 1937.
Congressional Record, 75th Congress, 82, pt. 2, 2nd Session, 1937.
Congressional Record, 75th Congress, 83, pt. 7, 3rd Session 1938.

About the Author

Bruce Newman was born and raised in Wilmington, Delaware. After serving three years in the U. S. Army, he graduated from University of Delaware with a B.A. degree in Philosophy and Political Science and from the University of Dallas M.A. and Ph.D. in Politics. Bruce teaches political science at Western Oklahoma State College in Altus, Oklahoma, where he resides with his wife Alice and three children. He is also an adjunct scholar at the Oklahoma Council of Public Affairs. Bruce's articles have been published in the *Wall Street Journal* and *Perspective: A Public Policy Journal of the Oklahoma Council of Public Affairs.*

www.ingramcontent.com/pod-product-compliance
Lightning Source LLC
Chambersburg PA
CBHW021852300426
44115CB00005B/122